THE STORY OF SPENCER W. KIMBALL:
A SHORT MAN, A LONG STRIDE

THE STORY OF SPENCER W. KIMBALL: A SHORT MAN, A LONG STRIDE

Edward L. Kimball and Andrew E. Kimball, Jr.

Design/Illustration, S. Thompson Associates

Bookcraft
Salt Lake City, Utah

Library of Congress Catalog Card Number: 85-73002
ISBN 0-88494-584-7

First Printing, 1985

Printed in the United States of America

PREFACE

The biography *Spencer W. Kimball,* published in 1977, received an enthusiastic reception from people who started out dutifully to read about the President of the Church and found in the book a man they could identify with. Spencer Kimball never made any pretence of perfection. In fact he fully realized his inadequacies. But he overcame great difficulties in life because of his simple, deep commitment to the Lord and his Church. He became the sort of person the Lord could use to bless His people.

President Kimball once went to Cleveland to speak to a large public gathering. While there he spent some time with a non-Mormon cousin. Afterward the cousin commented to Arthur Haycock, President Kimball's secretary, "You Mormons should make my cousin Spencer a Saint, like Saint Peter." Arthur found the idea of calling the President Saint Spencer amusing and reported it to him. Though usually quick to see the humor in things, this time the President said seriously, "You know, Arthur, no one can make you a Saint. You have to make yourself one."

This, then, is the story of a man who made himself a Saint.

THE STORY OF SPENCER W. KIMBALL: A SHORT MAN, A LONG STRIDE

In 1980 several Church leaders returned together from the St. Louis area conference on an airplane. Elder Ronald Poelman got up to walk in the aisle. President Kimball caught his arm and asked, "Where are you going?"

"I was just stretching my legs."

"You don't need to do that; they're long enough already. It's little people like me who need to stretch their legs."

Only five feet six at his tallest, with short legs, Spencer Woolley Kimball often said, "I sit tall but I stand short. I got the Woolley genes." His mother, Olive Woolley, stood just five feet tall, a shy girl with a round, pretty face, clear skin, blue eyes, and reddish hair. His father, Andrew, on the other hand, was a slender man six feet tall. Spencer may have got his mother's build but he had his father's dark eyes and black hair.

Spencer was born March 28, 1895, the sixth of eleven children, in a modest brick home in the northwest part of Salt Lake City. Andrew Kimball, one of the younger sons of Heber C. Kimball, had earlier worked at farming, tanning leather, building, and railroading, but now he drove a wagon around Utah and southern Idaho selling things like soap, salt, and candy. This was a good kind of work for him, because he was also a mission president of the Indian Territory Mission (where Oklahoma is today). After working for a time to support his family, he would go by train to visit his missionaries. Eleven years earlier, as a young married man, he had been called to leave Olive and a baby to spend two difficult years in the Indian Territory as a missionary himself, suffering from malaria while he taught the gospel to Indians and white people. After his mission the First Presidency had asked Andrew to continue on, serving as president on a part-time basis, and that is what he was doing when Spencer came into the family.

When Spencer was not quite three years old the Presidency of the Church released his father as mission president and asked him to go to the Gila Valley in southeastern Arizona to become the president of the St. Joseph Stake. This calling, to move his family to Arizona, would not necessarily end after a two- or three-year term. To be called as a stake president then meant a permanent move. Andrew served as stake president for the rest of his life, twenty-six years.

Southeastern Arizona was new country. Mormon settlers had established farming towns in the Gila Valley just a few years earlier, and people still remembered the Indian raids, when several people had been killed. Olive wept at the thought of leaving her home and her relatives; Andrew had no great enthusiasm for moving to the Arizona desert, either. But they had received the call from President Wilford Woodruff, a prophet of God, and they loyally accepted the assignment to start life all over again in the desert.

Rain fell as they boarded the train, leaving behind a cluster of well-wishers huddled under dripping umbrellas. A hundred miles along the way their train stopped because a large rock had rolled from the mountain onto the track, and men had to move it before the train could go on. After the rain let up they kept the windows of the train open for fresh air, and smoke and cinders from the engine blew in. The swaying of the train made almost all the family, including Spencer, motion sick, as the train klop-klopped over mountains and desert to their new home in the Gila Valley.

They had feared a desert of cactus, snakes, and scorpions, but they found that in the Gila Valley itself irrigation water taken out of the river made the land green and productive. When they arrived in the Mormon town of Thatcher on the fourth day of travel, a crowd of townspeople met them to sing welcome to the new stake president. But the wind blew so hard that, instead of singing, the people just showered the Kimballs with rose petals.

The little town had no real train station and no platform, so the train men just pushed the Kimballs' crated furniture off onto the ground. Some things Olive had carefully packed broke. After a few days Andrew found and rented a three-room house made of mud bricks. Because the house was too small for the family, now eight people, Andrew pitched a big six-room white tent just outside. They called it "The White House" and lived in it for several years. Neither the house nor the tent had plumbing. They relied on an outhouse and a well, as their neighbors did.

The good people of Thatcher gave the Kimball family ten acres of land and helped dig out the greasewood, chaparral, and hundreds of mesquite trees to make farming possible. Gordon and Del, Spencer's two older brothers, were only ten and seven, but they worked with the grown-ups at farming. Spencer, for the time being, just played on his broom-stick horse. His turn to work came later.

Spencer grew up adoring his father and loved to be with him. Andrew got his son a boy-size pitchfork to use and Spencer did not even mind the farm chores too much when he could work beside Pa. Spencer considered his father the most important man in Arizona. In many ways Spencer came to be much like him—each was an important person in the Church and community—but they differed markedly in temperament. Andrew carried himself with dignity, a rather formal man; Spencer had a gift for easy geniality.

Andrew worked at various occupations in Arizona—
farming; selling farm equipment, suits, patent
medicines, Bibles, and insurance; representing the
railroad; serving in the state legislature; and
contracting to build a stretch of railroad. He spent so
much of his time looking after the welfare of the
several thousand Church members in his stake,
however, that he earned only just enough for his
family to get by. Spencer wore hand-me-downs and
learned to straighten old bent nails and use them over
again. Though most of the neighbors lived the same
way, one of Spencer's friends had a father who ran a
candy store, and Spencer envied him.

Andrew and Olive thought that Thatcher should be a
progressive town, so they sacrificed to set the example.
Though they scrimped in other ways, the Kimball
home was one of the first to have a piano, to install
running water, and to get a bathtub. Andrew and his
sons planted varieties of fruit trees no one else had and
exotic shade trees like cypress and eucalyptus. At that
time young people started full-time work early in life;
few even graduated from high school. But Andrew
kept the struggling Church-run high school going by
urging people to support it and send their children
there for education, as Andrew sent all his.

When Andrew travelled he always promoted Arizona.
He carried with him documents proving how big the

corn and sweet potatoes and peaches grew in Arizona. And he would tell people that they ought to move to Arizona, because of the great opportunities there for someone with determination.

Thatcher had its share of people the children found intriguing—the mailman with one ear missing; the one black woman in town; the neighbor with hair so bushy that the children would joke whenever they lost something, "It must have been lost in Brother _____'s hair"; the man who capered about at the baseball games like a monkey; the eccentric squatter who lived by the cemetery in a small shack and bore terrible scars from a shovel fight over water rights.

I n this desert country, rain was critical. If it did not rain for a long time the river nearly dried up and the canals could not bring enough water to the fields. Then, to save the trees at least, Spencer would dip water from a barrel he had filled from the trickle in the Union Canal. If water sloshed on him he didn't mind. Members of the stake would join in fasting and prayer for rain.

Spencer knew early about fasting and prayer, though it took a while to get things straight. At about four, he asked his mother, "Ma, can I have a piece of bread and butter to fast on?"

Prayers received answers. After little three-year-old
Leo Cluff, a rancher's son, had been gored by a stray
cow, the doctor poked his intestines back in and sewed
him up. The doctor did his best but expected the boy
to die. The family called Andrew Kimball, who
blessed Leo by the power of the priesthood. Spencer,
five, came with his father and added his prayers. The
next day, when the Cluffs did not bring the boy's body
to town for burial, the doctor drove out to the ranch in
his buggy. To his amazement Leo was healing.

Spencer walked with his mother up the dusty road to
the bishop's house. "Why are we going?" asked

Spencer. "To take the tithing eggs," she replied, and explained that tithing was a tenth of what they gathered. And when Spencer and Helen, his little sister, took the potatoes from their own potato patch in a little red wagon and sold them to the hotel kitchen, their father asked, "What are you going to do with the money?" They told him their plans for ice cream, candy, Christmas presents. He said, "You haven't forgotten the Lord, have you? The Lord has blessed us and we always give back one tenth to the Lord." And when the boys cut hay, Andrew told them to be sure to get each tenth wagon load, which went to the tithing barn, from the best part of the field.

The Kimballs always went to church. On Saturday nights Spencer's mother bathed him in a tub of water that had been heated on the wood stove. He hated the scrubbing almost as much as he loved his mother. In Sunday meetings he sometimes slept with his head resting in his mother's soft lap. He heard the preaching, but he also liked to watch the people. One of the men continuously wiggled his fingers as he prayed, and the boys all peeked and giggled. If testimony meeting lagged, the short white-haired stake patriarch would burst out into a song until everyone joined him. When the sacrament was served, everyone drank from the same two-handled goblets; it seemed to Spencer that they all turned the goblet around to drink from the same "unused" place, by the handle.

On Spencer's eighth birthday his father baptized him in the big metal vat that they sometimes used as a bathtub. He was pleased to be a full Church member. But four years later someone suggested the baptism might not be quite right, because Andrew had not gone down into the water with his son; so, just to be sure, Spencer was baptized again in the Union Canal, where the boys sometimes went swimming.

Spencer's mother thought children were not mature enough for school until they were seven, so when Spencer started he was a year behind the other children. At school children sometimes wanted to know his middle name, but he didn't usually like to tell them it was Woolley, because they made fun of it. Instead he called himself plain Spencer Kimball, but never Spence, always Spencer, because that is what his parents called him.

At noon he usually ran the three blocks from school to home to pump water for the animals, feed the pigs, and eat his lunch. One day his mother said, "What are you doing home at recess? It's not noon yet." He ran back to school in a panic and found his classmates already inside from the brief recess. Everyone laughed—except the teacher, who took that occasion to tell the class that Spencer was ahead of all the other students in the second grade and would be moved up to be with the children his own age.

At recess and after school the children played games—marbles, pop-the-whip, leapfrog, and kick-the-can. Spencer chased one chubby girl with caterpillers to hear her scream. Another time he doused Ella Tyler with a bucket of water. She later said, "The only reason Spencer Kimball lived to become a General Authority is that I am a slow runner." Sometimes things got rough. Spencer didn't fight often, but once when the governor was visiting Spencer's father and Spencer was left to play with the governor's son, Sandy, they got into a fight and Spencer bloodied Sandy's nose. Everyone was upset except the governor, who said (to Spencer's great relief) that his son had to learn to take care of himself.

One day the community had a picnic at Cluffs' ranch and after lunch went swimming in the pond. Spencer didn't know how to swim, so he rode on his father's back out into the deep water. When they got back to shallower water Spencer said, "I can get off here, Pa," and started to walk to shore. His father swam away and just then Spencer stepped into a big hole and went under. He lost his breath and started to drown. He wanted to scream but couldn't. His father shouted, "Spencer!" and got back to him in time to drag him, coughing and spitting, to shore. Even though he later learned to swim, he never really got over his fear of deep water.

Work on the farm never ended. Girls helped in the house; boys worked outside. For Spencer there were weeds to chop, garden to tend, cows to milk, fence to build, hay to stack. One sweltering afternoon his older brothers Gordon and Del were pitching hay up onto the wagon for Spencer to tromp. Hearing the church bell calling children to Primary, Spencer called down to them, "I've got to go to Primary." They answered, "You're not going to Primary today." He said, "If Pa were here he'd let me go." "Well, Pa is not here and you're not going." They kept throwing hay up but heard no tromping. Then they saw Spencer half way across the field running to Primary. He said later, "I've always gotten lots of credit from people for being a very good Primary boy," but in truth the cool chapel promised a lot more comfort than tromping hay in the sun.

Spencer had to feed and water the animals. When his father heard the pigs squealing he would say, "Spencer, haven't you fed the pigs yet?" The family had as many as fifty pigs at one time, and Spencer could never satisfy them for long. He often said, when he did not grow very tall, "The thing that stunted my growth was carrying all those five-gallon cans full of slop to the hogs."

And the nine cows never seemed to get full of water. The pump handle burned his hands in summer and froze them in winter. To fill the time, he counted the strokes of the pump, he said the ABCs forward and backward, he said the times tables and the Articles of Faith. And while he milked the cows he would memorize scriptures or the words of hymns. Sometimes he squirted milk in the mouths of the cats that gathered around. Anything to pass the time.

Once Spencer's father took him to Utah to attend general conference. They visited more uncles and aunts and cousins in Salt Lake City than he could imagine. Andrew seemed proud of him and took him in to meet the Presidency of the Church. On the way home they stopped in San Francisco. There Spencer had his first experience with an amusement park and the sea and cable-cars and Chinatown. Though he had had a wonderful five-week adventure, as the train chugged the last miles toward Thatcher he danced in the aisle and wept for joy to be home again.

Sickness plagued people. Contaminated water spread typhoid fever, and flies spread other diseases. Spencer spent seven weeks in bed with a "light case" of typhoid fever; many in his town died that same spring. Three of his sisters died of various causes while he was just a boy.

One day at breakfast his brothers started to laugh at Spencer. "Look at Spunk," they teased. One side of his face sagged. He couldn't blink his eye or pucker his lips to whistle. The family was frightened and the doctor couldn't figure out the problem. His father planned to send him to doctors in Salt Lake City to see if they could find out what was wrong, but (Spencer later said) "Unfortunately my face got well and I could not go to Utah."

When Spencer was eleven, his mother, Olive, became seriously ill while expecting her twelfth child. Andrew took her to Salt Lake City for treatment, but her strength dwindled day by day. A month later the Kimball children were called out of school by their bishop. He told them, as gently as he could, "Children, your mother is dead." It struck like a thunderbolt! Spencer ran out of sight to be alone as he sobbed, tears flooding forth until he felt drained dry, his heart nearly bursting. His world had revolved around his small, kindly mother, who never said a mean thing about anyone. When he would come home from school the first thing he would do as he hung his cap over the wash dish was call, "Ma! Ma!" until he found her. When she asked what he wanted, he said, "Nothing," and ran out to play. He just wanted to know that she was there. Now she was gone.

For five days, waiting for the train to come from Salt Lake City, Spencer felt empty. He wept while milking the cows and doing his chores. He didn't go to school; he didn't go to church; he didn't play. He waited. Finally his father arrived, bringing Olive's body in a coffin, and the sad funeral could take place. They lowered her coffin slowly and filled the grave carefully, for gentle Olive had often said she could not stand the thought of rocks and gravel clattering on her casket.

Ruth, thirteen, dropped out of school to take care of the family, but the children needed a grown-up mother. Before Olive died, she and Andrew had talked about the children's need for a mother and Olive had approved of Josie Cluff, who was her age. Now Andrew took the children aside and made sure that they had no objection. After a few months

Andrew married Josephine Cluff, whose own two children were grown up.

Spencer always called Josie "Mother"; Olive was his only "Ma." Josie kept a clean house and cooked well, but she was a no-nonsense person, not so gentle as Olive. She saw it her duty to take on the task of rearing her friend's half-grown family. And though neither Josie nor Andrew nor the children found it easy, they determinedly made it work.

Spencer grew up physically strong, proud of his ability to do a hard day's work. He also learned the value of working carefully. He served his father as business secretary, learning to handle correspondence and to type accurately with two fingers. His father expected precision from his sons. When they painted the buggy, the hairline stripe had to be even and straight. When they complained at his insistence on careful detail in cabinet making he explained, "People won't ask how long it took to make a cupboard, but how well it is made."

One of the horses got tangled in a wire fence and suffered deep cuts on its shoulder. With no one else there to help, Spencer washed the wounds, put liniment on, and tried to sew it closed with a large needle and ordinary thread. The horse kicked at Spencer and bit him. With mixed emotions toward the injured animal, Spencer showed his sister how to twist the horse's lip, causing enough pain to distract its attention away from the sewing. He hurt the animal to save it.

Spencer watched other boys steal watermelons from a neighbor's patch or slash fifty melons open to rot and then run, but he thought that was not fair. Sometimes they would kill birds with a slingshot to test their aim, but he remembered a Sunday school song, "Don't Kill the Little Birds," and refused to participate. Other boys would play mean pranks, but he would not participate with them. One evening he pulled Charlie McDonald's shirt tight around his neck and Charlie blacked out, but that was not intentional harm, just horseplay.

Spencer and some of the boys borrowed a horse and an old buggy to use when their science class at school went on a field trip. On the rough road a buggy spring broke. The next day Spencer explained to his friends, "We ought to all pitch in some money to pay for the broken spring," but no one offered to help. He persuaded them, saying, "That spring's going to be paid for, if I have to do it myself."

As a deacon Spencer took his priesthood seriously. He attended the Monday night meetings regularly, except when they were cancelled for the summer months for the benefit of the farmers. He faithfully fulfilled his assignments. When he went to collect fast offerings (usually squash, honey, or bottles of fruit, but occasionally cash), his father let him use a horse and buggy.

After Sunday School class one day when Spencer was fourteen, the Sunday School superintendent stopped him. Spencer expected a scolding for teasing the girls, but to his surprise the man asked him to teach a Sunday School class himself. Of course Spencer accepted the assignment; he had a commitment to keep.

About this time Spencer heard Brigham Young's daughter Susa Young Gates speak in stake conference. When she asked who in the large congregation had read the whole Bible Spencer craned his neck but could see only a few hands go up. He took the challenge. As soon as he got home he lighted the coal-oil lamp in his unfinished attic room and started to read, "In the beginning. . . ." A year later, after plowing through the whole Bible a few pages a day, whether he understood what he was reading or not, he finished with a sense of satisfaction for meeting the challenge.

After Spencer graduated from grade school, he attended the Church-sponsored high school they called the Academy. There were fifty-six in his entering class, but more than half of them

In the beginning God created the heaven and the earth

dropped out without graduating. Some had to go to work; others got married. When class elections were held, one of Spencer's friends nominated him to be freshman class president; then another friend moved to close the ballot. Since no one seemed to know what to do next, Spencer was elected. And each year his classmates reelected him. He told them, "There's no reason to change horses in the middle of the stream."

Spencer was a good student. He also found ways to make school life exciting. One time Spencer and a friend made "rotten egg gas" in the school's chemistry laboratory, and classes in the whole school had to be dismissed for the day. He received his only B in chemistry; the rest of his grades were A's.

Sometimes Spencer and his friends went to silent movies at the local theater or a play put on by the ward, but mostly they made their own fun by having parties at homes, at church, and at school. Spencer always added life to the party. He told stories, he

25

generated ideas, and he played popular tunes on the piano for them to sing to.

At fourteen Spencer and some friends formed an orchestra. Spencer was not very good at first, having learned to play the piano mostly on his own, with only a few formal piano lessons, but he got better as time went on and earned a little spending money that way. It meant late hours. One night at midnight, after a dance, Spencer took Ella Tyler home and they stood outside, talking. After what seemed only a short time they heard the clock in the house strike two. Shocked, Ella slipped inside and Spencer hurried home. The next morning Ella's mother admitted she had put the clock ahead so that Ella and Spencer wouldn't stay outside any longer.

Spencer loved sports, but the school offered little formal coaching. Once his school sent a group of boys, who had not much training, to another school for a track meet. When it came to the mile run the other boys were too tired, so the coach said to Spencer, "I guess we'll let you run the mile." Spencer got on his mark, and when the signal sounded he raced off with the others. He had not trained for such a long race and he hurt, his breath coming in gasps, but he was determined to give the race his best effort. On the home stretch things seemed to blur. All he could see was a crowd waving and shouting. He fell across the line exhausted. Friends slapped him on the back, congratulating him, "You came in third, anyway!" Spencer smiled at the congratulations, knowing that there had only been three boys in the race.

Spencer liked to play basketball better than anything, even better than eating, and especially better than working. After school he would often play so long that when he got home he could expect a scolding from his stepmother because neighbors were waiting to buy milk from cows that weren't milked yet.

During his senior year the Academy basketball team, on which he starred as the youngest and smallest but quickest member, played a challenge game against the University of Arizona in a makeshift gymnasium in the basement of the Thatcher chapel. His team regularly played there and knew how to shoot the ball low to miss the overhanging beams. With that advantage the Academy boys defeated the university team that had been almost too proud to play the high school boys. Because Spencer had led the team to victory, his teammates paraded him around on their shoulders. The next night, on a regulation floor, the university team won. Even so, nothing could take away the thrill of that earlier victory over the haughty university team.

Just before April Fools' Day the school principal said to the assembled students, "We'll hold school tomorrow as usual; there'll be no tricks." Taking the warning as a dare, Spencer and his friends secretly organized an outing. On April first nearly all the boys in the small school failed to show up: they went off to the mountain with a picnic lunch to ride the lumber flume, a water-filled slide that the saw mill high up on the mountain used to float boards down. The next day the boys found they had all been expelled. They wondered what to do. They wandered about, talking. Then they had a photographer take a portrait of the whole thirty-two of them in front of a Bull Durham tobacco sign. Finally one of the teachers persuaded Spencer that, as the leader, he should go and apologize to the principal and the teachers. He did that and the boys were allowed back in school in time to graduate.

After graduation Spencer and several of his friends planned to go on to college, but at the graduation ceremony his father, who was conducting the service, shocked Spencer by publicly announcing that Spencer would not be going to college, but on a mission instead. His friends thought Spencer would faint. He had not been thinking much about a mission, because in those days missionaries were usually older men. At first he hesitated, but he quickly got used to the idea, and when the formal call came from Church headquarters in Salt Lake City he readily accepted it.

In gathering money for his mission in the fall, Spencer sold his spirited black horse and worked during the summer on a dairy near the copper-mining town of Globe, Arizona, doing very hard work. After only about six hours in bed, he and the other dairy workers got up around 8:00 A.M. and ate, then fed the cows and washed bottles and milked cows until noon. In the afternoon they separated the cream and fed the calves and cleaned the barn and worked at chores like cutting wood. Then late at night they milked the cows again, finishing about two in the morning. The scalding hot water they used for washing bottles and equipment softened their fingers, and then the milking of so many cows by hand made their fingers sore. When they walked to church on Sunday their swollen hands sometimes hurt so much that they would hold them up in the air to let the blood drain out—unless someone came along who would see the curious parade.

Some tough boys also worked on the dairy and once beat up Spencer's friend, but when the boss, a cigar-smoking non-Mormon, found out he fired the rowdies. At the end of the summer, to Spencer's great surprise, the boss had a party for him and gave him a gold watch to take on his mission.

Spencer went on his mission at 19, younger than most missionaries. Shortly after he arrived in Missouri the mission president assigned him and his companion to start knocking on doors in the country outside Jefferson City. As it got late the first day they started asking for a place to sleep. Family after family turned them away until things looked desperate. Finally, near midnight, they walked toward a light in a house back in the trees. A gruff man said they could stay for the night and showed them to a bed in the attic. The next morning they found themselves covered with bites from bugs and the bed spotted with blood, but they remained grateful for the man's hospitality and even for the breakfast of blood pudding he offered.

Every night as they worked out in the country they had to rely on people's generosity. One time, after they had preached in a schoolhouse in the woods and asked for a bed, a family of eight led him and his companion down a seemingly endless trail to a one-room shack. The mother and five children disappeared into a loft; the father and one son shared a cot; and the missionaries slept in the only bed in the house. The family couldn't have treated a king better; they gave the very best they had.

During Spencer's mission his closest sister, Ruth, died. She was the one who as a child had pooled money with him for Christmas presents and had stayed home to tend the family when their mother died. To Spencer it was almost as though his mother had died again. He felt so sorry for himself that for a few days he moped around, neglecting his missionary work. Generally however, Spencer was a diligent and creative missionary. When a reluctant woman was about to shut the door on the two missionaries he saw her piano and said, "Isn't that a Kimball piano? That's my name, too. Would you like for me to play you a song?" She did; and he did, making another friend.

His mission president assigned Spencer to the St. Louis area and put him in charge of the twenty-five other missionaries there, all older than he was. Spencer worried about his ability to handle the assignment, but he proved to be a good leader, recording 3,844 nonmember contacts during the first half of 1916 and an average of fourteen meetings a week.

Sometimes they held meetings on the street corner, preaching to whoever would stop to listen. One time after the missionaries had sung a song and prayed, Elder Hawkes waved his long arms about and said in a loud voice, "If you will all give me your attention, we will begin our meeting." Spencer had to laugh, because there was no one within a block of them to listen.

During the bitter winter cold, Spencer and his companion were running out of money. They prayed earnestly for help. The day they put their last quarter into a metered gas stove a letter arrived from one of the boys Spencer had known at the dairy. The boy wanted nothing to do with the Church, but his letter contained two dollars, "the most welcome two dollars I have ever seen," said Spencer.

When Spencer left on his mission he already had a good knowledge of the gospel from growing up in the Church and from reading the scriptures, but his service strengthened his commitment. At first he had wondered whether he was really sure, but when the Spirit moved him he could say with conviction, "I know the gospel is true."

Having a testimony did not by itself guarantee faithfulness. When his mission ended and he returned home, he went off to the University of Arizona to start college. Without family encouragement or Church responsibility he found himself slipping into bad habits, sleeping late on Sunday and missing meetings. But he soon realized by himself what was happening and he made a conscious decision to be faithful in attending meetings; he realized that if he did not, he might just slide out of the Church. He found that the more he served in the Church, the more spiritual confirmation he had that he was doing the right thing.

The following summer he got a job in Los Angeles in the railroad freight yards working fourteen-hour days wheeling heavy loads, up to a thousand pounds, on a hand truck. He boarded with his sister Clare, and after work he often walked the several miles to her house to save the dime streetcar fare for college expenses. He carried a book and read as he walked along.

He did not so much mind the hard work, but he did mind the other workers' swearing and telling dirty stories. When he and a friend could not take it any longer they went to the boss to say they had to quit. When the boss learned why, he asked them to wait a little. Shortly afterward he gave them an easier job at better pay as checkers. One of their first tasks in the new job was to help clean out a freight car which had carried a load of chocolate. The car had been left on a siding in the hot desert sun, and the cargo had dripped and formed "icicles." For once they had their fill of chocolate.

Later that summer Spencer got a job on a ranch near home, mining for water. He and his stepbrother blasted and dug a hole deeper and deeper, hoping to find water. One day on the ranch Spencer read in the weekly newspaper that a young woman named Camilla Eyring would be coming to teach high school at the Academy in Thatcher. Spencer had barely met her at a dance before his mission, but when he read about her now he had a feeling that this was the young woman he would marry.

He figured out a way to meet her again. Soon after school started in the fall he was waiting at her bus stop

when she came to catch the little bus to her parents'
home in Pima, the next town. He introduced himself.
"You're Miss Eyring, aren't you? I'm Spencer Kimball.
I'm going to Pima to visit a friend. Do you mind
riding together?" She didn't mind. They spent the trip
trying to impress one another, talking about
Shakespeare and poetry and high-brow things. When
they arrived, Spencer helped her off the bus and said,
"May I come see you some time?" She said, of course,
that she would be delighted.

The very next evening Camilla was dressed in a
kimono, hair in curlers, getting ready to go to a dance
with a date when Spencer arrived unannounced. She
quickly got ready and, thinking he might stay just a
short while, sat on the porch with him. But he did not
go and did not go and seemed ready to spend the whole
evening visiting. She didn't want to discourage him, so
finally she said in desperation, "A group of us are going
to Safford to a dance. Would you like to go along?" He
said yes. And then when her date and another couple
came driving up she hurried out to the car and
apologized: "This friend just dropped over; would it be
all right if he went to the dance with us?" Her date
didn't dare say no, so Spencer happily joined the
group. Camilla's date was so angry that he drove "like
the devil was after him." When they got to the dance
he avoided her the whole evening; he wouldn't dance

with her even once. Though she was sorry for having manipulated the situation, she didn't feel too sad, because Spencer kept her dancing all evening.

The first World War was going on and Spencer's father urged him to volunteer. But Spencer had been away on his mission for two years and wanted to get more schooling first, if he could. Shortly after getting acquainted with Camilla, Spencer left for Utah to attend Brigham Young University. He and Camilla started exchanging letters that got progressively friendlier.

When Spencer arrived in Provo, Utah, he got off the interurban railway from Salt Lake City and looked up the street toward the mountain. He saw an imposing white building that he figured must be BYU, so he carried his heavy suitcase up the slope more than a mile until he neared the building. Then he noticed some men in coveralls working on the grounds who looked a bit peculiar. Finally he remembered that Provo had two major institutions, BYU and the state insane asylum. But rather than retreat he put his suitcase behind a bush and walked right into the building, as if he owned the place, and got a drink. Then he turned around and lugged his suitcase back to town and asked directions to BYU. He was so embarrassed about his mistake that he did not tell anyone for a long time about the "school" he tried to get into.

With so many young men gone off to war the classes at BYU were small. He wrote to Camilla, "I was the only member in the public speaking class so I get individual instruction. I can now breathe clear down to my toes, can roar like a lion or squeak like a mouse. I can gesticulate till you'd think I was hammering or pitching hay or etc., etc. There were two of us in Math, 4 in Hist., about 6 in Theology. . . . I like all my Profs fine but _____ and I can't hardly stand him. Today he had a dirtier shirt than mine and wore the trousers and shoes he wore while milking the cows."

After only a few days at school he received a notice that he should take a physical examination to see if he was fit for military service. When the doctors found him in perfect health he left for home, expecting to be sent off in the next group of soldiers gathered from his community.

Returning home meant interrupting his education and going off to war, but it also meant that he could see Camilla again much sooner than he had expected. She met him at the train. The army group he expected to join had left early. While he waited for the army to organize another group he spent all the time he could with Camilla. Her family was pleased with Spencer, and every night Camilla's mother invited him to stay for dinner. She made cream pies especially for him. Spencer and Camilla spent the evenings together until late, swinging on the gate or walking in the moonlight. Then Spencer would sleep all morning the next day, while poor Camilla had to get up early and teach school. When Camilla fell asleep in class the children snickered, because they knew what was going on—they could see Spencer, fresh and bright-eyed, waiting outside to take Camilla home in his father's Chevrolet.

One night, after only a few weeks of intense courting, as they walked along the railroad grade in the moonlight Spencer and Camilla decided to get married. They discussed the possibility that Spencer might be killed in the war, but Camilla agreed to take that chance. They would have liked to travel to Salt Lake City to be married in the temple, but the school would not let her go long enough for the trip; besides, they did not have money for such travel.

They kept their plans a secret from everyone except their families, because they were determined to avoid a shivaree. Shivarees were common practice, teasing the newlyweds with noise or even kidnapping the bride for the evening. That was one of the local customs they hated.

On Friday, November 16, 1917, the day of the wedding, Spencer drove Camilla home after school, then rushed to get ready. He undressed and stepped into the metal tub before he realized he had forgotten the water, so he had to call for his stepmother, Josie, to bring him a bucket of hot water and hand it in to him.

In the meantime Camilla panicked. She was about to marry a young man she had known only a few weeks, who had no job, and who would leave for the army at any time. But she had committed herself, and there was something special about this Spencer. She didn't have much time for tears as she hurried to get the living room of her parents' ramshackle home ready for the wedding. She and her mother used tree branches as decorations to camouflage bad spots in the wallpaper. She also worried that the dress she planned to wear, a pink party dress she had made at school, was not right for a wedding.

Spencer arrived in his khaki uniform, and while they waited the young couple found a quiet spot to be alone. Camilla's little brother Henry wandered in and saw them kissing. He ran out, flustered, saying, "I'll be as silent as the tomb!" Kindly old Bishop Merrell performed the ceremony for them, and then the small group of immediate family members who had gathered ate cake and drank cocoa to celebrate this hurried marriage.

Spencer and Camilla spent the weekend together on the Eyring ranch, but early Monday morning Camilla had to go right back to work. They made their first home with his parents, because they had no money. The situation was anything but comfortable; Josie expected Camilla to do her full load of chores at home in addition to teaching at the Academy.

They borrowed a hundred dollars and moved into half of a two-room house occupied by Spencer's sister, her husband, and her colicky baby, who cried all the time. Though the rooms were divided only by blankets, at least it was better than living with parents-in-law. On top of it all, Camilla very soon became pregnant and didn't feel well.

Camilla's job brought in seventy-five dollars a month and Spencer worked for two dollars a day helping farmers. Then when it looked as though the army would not call Spencer up for a while, he got a regular job in the bank at the same salary as Camilla received. Some of his friends earned twice that much, but employers did not know how long Spencer would be around. Anyway, he joked, it was easier to pay tithing when you didn't have so much income. He used seven dollars of his first regular salary money to buy Camilla a simple wedding ring.

They lived thriftily, and by March they had worked themselves out of debt and rented a tiny, unfurnished house for six dollars a month. They got some old furniture from relatives and used an orange crate for a cupboard. They had no running water, but that was not unusual for the time. They loved being on their own and having the privacy the little house afforded.

By June Camilla's school was out and they had saved enough money to travel to Salt Lake City by train to get to the temple. She was awkwardly pregnant and irritable, but the trip was important to them both, so that their marriage could be sealed for eternity.

During her last month of pregnancy, in the heat of an Arizona August, Camilla bounced over rough roads in a Model T Ford, completing her school contract by visiting students who were working on projects at home. Finally in late August she went into labor with her first baby. The delivery proved extremely difficult. Spencer held her hand the whole time, trying to comfort her. But after all the difficulty they had a big baby boy they named Spencer LeVan. At first they were worried because LeVan's head seemed all out of shape and they feared he might be mentally retarded, but soon his head took normal shape and he proved to be an unusually bright boy who started school in the second grade.

World War I ended with the Armistice of November 11, 1918, and Spencer no longer had to worry about when he might be called up to serve in the army. Now that they had a child, Spencer looked for extra work. He started playing the piano in a dance band and kept books for a store, in addition to his job in the bank and his Church position as stake clerk (which at that time was a paid part-time job). Financially things improved, but with four jobs Spencer did not get enough sleep and his eyes started to bother him so that he became cranky with his family. He decided that the extra money was just not worth what it was doing to his home life, so he quit the dance band, with its late night hours, and things got better again. He could handle the other three jobs.

About four years after they were married Spencer and Camilla had saved enough money to buy a new car and make the down payment on their first home, a little frame house with kitchen, living-dining room, bedroom and bath, and a sleeping porch for the hot Arizona nights. Spencer planted a palm tree in the front yard to grow up with his family.

When Spencer needed to have a cow delivered to the Eyring farm, ten miles away, he hired a bashful twelve-year-old boy to trail the cow along behind his donkey. The boy didn't get back until late at night. He expected about $1.50, since grown men were getting $3 a day, but Spencer said, "I knew you would do the job right," and handed him five dollars.

A few years after the war ended there was a period of economic trouble in the country. Because the bank in which Spencer worked was having troubles, the employees took a cut in pay. But at home things were better. After some miscarriages, Camilla bore a second child, a lovely blond blue-eyed girl they named Olive Beth, after Spencer's mother.

In 1923 the bank failed and Spencer found himself suddenly out of a job. Not only that, but they had invested all their savings in the bank and they lost everything they had saved in six years and had to start over again. But two things he still had: experience and a good reputation. Right away a store and two other banks offered him jobs. He chose to go to work for a bank as chief teller. He earned the same salary and had a more responsible position than before.

Spencer found that the other two tellers had what they called a "petty cash box," into which they would put money if they had extra at the end of the day or from which they would take money to even up their accounts if they were a little short. Spencer asked them, "Why do you do that? Why don't you make your accounts balance exactly?" "No one could handle as many transactions as we have to in a day without being off a little sometimes," they laughed. Spencer took it as a challenge. If they would never make change from his window without checking with him, he would make his books and cash come out even every day. Sure enough, with care, day after day Spencer's books balanced to the penny, and soon the other two tellers learned that if they were careful they too could balance every day.

As a boy Spencer had learned to type with two fingers when he wrote letters for his father. Now he decided to learn to type the more efficient way, with all ten fingers. He bought a typing book and came early every day to practice on an office typewriter until he could type quickly. Later, in business and Church work he found the skill invaluable. He would stand at his business office counter, his fingers plunging up and down. Or as he travelled on Church affairs he perched a portable typewriter on his knees.

In 1922 Spencer's stepmother, Josie, died of heart trouble and his father, Andrew, married again. But Andrew was in his sixties and soon his health failed too. In 1924 Andrew went to Salt Lake City, where better medical care was available. His health continued to get worse. When it looked like the end was near, Spencer took leave from his job to go and be with his father. He sat through long nights holding his father's hand. Andrew suffered a great deal, throwing his hands and pounding the bed, moaning and crying out, "Oh! My! Oh, my God! How long? Oh, Father, let me die!" Spencer suffered in watching his father die slowly, but he stood loyally by. Finally Andrew's body rested.

Church President Heber J. Grant, who had been a life-long friend of Andrew's, travelled with Spencer to bring Andrew's body to Arizona for the funeral. All the Primary children in the stake lined up to see the body of this man who had been stake president for twenty-six years. Their teachers said they should never forget him. Spencer managed a brave front until his father's casket was lowered into place next to his mother, and then he broke down and sobbed almost uncontrollably. Both of his parents and five sisters were gone. Spencer was twenty-nine.

President Grant called a special conference to present a new stake presidency while he was there. The new president, Harry Payne, wanted Spencer to be his counselor. Spencer's older brothers tried to intervene by pleading with President Grant, "It's a mistake to take so young a man and put all that responsibility on him." President Grant closed the discussion, saying, "Spencer has been called to this work, and he can do as he pleases about it." But Spencer never considered refusing the call. He had too much faith and commitment to the Church. He didn't know how well he would succeed, but he knew that he would never do less than his best in serving the Lord.

People saw this new stake leader as young, handsome, kind—everyone's friend, an extension of his father. He had a remarkable memory for people. A boy was greatly impressed when he and his parents, who lived in another town, met Spencer on the street one day. Spencer greeted them by name and insisted on buying them lemonade in the drug store.

Sitting on the stand as a stake visitor to the Eden Ward, he saw a group of five boys sitting on the front row, acting in unison. They crossed their legs at the same time, rubbed their chins, scratched their sides. Only after a long while did he realize that they were copying him, doing exactly what they saw him do. He took that as an object lesson to be a good example.

Spencer loved music. In addition to playing the piano, he led choirs and sang. One time in an adult music class at the Academy he and three friends started singing together as a quartet. They were good enough to be invited nearly everywhere in the Valley for parties, programs, and funerals. For some of their performances they wore fancy costumes like bull-fighters and called themselves the Conquistadores.

When a temple was built in Mesa, Arizona, the stake choir, in which Spencer sang, travelled to Mesa for the temple dedication. To get there they had to drive over treacherous mountain roads in a caravan so that on the steeper sections drivers could help one another push the cars, blocking the wheels with rocks when the travelers rested, mended tires, or cooled overheated engines. Despite the difficult travel, they were excited at having a temple so much nearer than Utah.

Camilla worked in Church callings and in the community. She helped organize the PTA and a public library in the town. She also managed to keep a clean house, cook, bake cinnamon rolls and bread, bottle fruit, and scrub clothes on a washboard with sweat dripping from her nose. She helped set the tone of the home with her love of books and ideas. A dictionary always lay within reach of the dining table, to resolve the frequent questions about words. She encouraged her brothers and sisters and children to study hard in school and get a good education. Most of them became teachers as she had been.

Camilla had the seven-dollar wedding ring Spencer bought with his first paycheck, but she had never had an engagement ring. One time they were shopping in a variety store and she spotted a toy "diamond" ring for ten cents. She said, "Oh, Spencer, I'm going to get myself an engagement ring." A friend, seeing the ring that evening, cried out excitedly, "Oh, Camilla, Spencer has bought you a new diamond!" She went on and on about how generous Spencer was. Camilla didn't say anything to embarrass the friend about her mistake, and later, after they had laughed about it, Spencer said, "Come on, Mama, I guess it is time we bought you a *real* engagement ring."

In 1927 two major events occurred. The Kimballs welcomed their third child, a boy they named Andrew Eyring, after Spencer's father. And Spencer started into business for himself when Bishop Joseph Greenhalgh persuaded him that the two of them could succeed in an insurance and real estate agency. The prospect of leaving the regular salary at the bank caused Spencer some hesitation, but the bank job did not offer him much chance of advancement. In his own business, success would depend, in a large measure at least, on him— his wits and his hard work.

Kimball-Greenhalgh opened for business in a tiny office in back of the bank. Spencer joked that from the beginning his business "operated close to a million dollars," only later explaining that since his office was just through the wall from the bank vault, his business was just a few feet from the million dollars. For advertising in local parades, they had a carpenter build a five-foot-high house model that fit right down over the cab of a pickup truck. Their sign, advertising insurance, said, "See us before you buy, burn, or die."

Things went well for a few years. Kimball-Greenhalgh grew enough to invest $20,000 in a subdivision planned for eighty-two houses. They put in sidewalks and curbs, planted trees, and began to sell lots. Then in 1929 the stock market crash threw the whole country into the Great Depression. Almost overnight, lots stopped selling and business ground nearly to a halt. Spencer decided to try selling some lots by auction. He hired a band and bought refreshments and prizes to give away and advertised heavily. But when the auction day came the Arizona skies, usually so blue, poured down rain. The band could not play, the decorations faded and blew away, and the people all stayed home. Not a single lot sold.

With cash scarce, people turned to trading. Store-keepers needed insurance, so they gave Kimball-Greenhalgh credit. When Camilla needed shoes for the children she would have to ask Spencer, "Which shoe store owes you money?" so that she could get shoes without cash. She longed for the days when she could just take money and buy wherever she wanted.

In 1930 the Kimballs had their fourth child, a red-haired boy they named Lawrence Edward—Edward after Camilla's father. When Camilla's sister heard that her father's name was to be second (and the first names of the other three children were Spencer, Olive, and Andrew, all from Spencer's side of the family), she protested. So they blessed the baby all over again and named him Edward Lawrence.

Spencer banked at the Bank of Safford, where he used to work. The several organizations whose accounts he kept banked there, too. He heard rumors floating around that the bank had problems, but his friend in the bank said there was nothing to the rumors. Then one day the bank closed its doors, taking with it thousands of dollars belonging to Kimball-Greenhalgh and the St. Joseph Stake and the various organizations of which he was secretary. What hurt especially was for Spencer to learn that one of the reasons the bank failed was that his friend stole $23,000 from the bank, living high on money he had taken from his neighbors' accounts.

While business was discouraging, he tried to be cheerful. He wrote to a friend about his troubles, "Business is offff, as you know; we are still hanging onnnn." Wise about people, Spencer understood that those who owe you money may hold it against you. One man who owed Spencer money began to avoid him. Spencer, true to his policy, kept after him until he paid, and as soon as the bill was paid the man became friendly again.

Kimball-Greenhalgh managed to stay above water. Spencer was a shrewd businessman, but fair. One time he had a house listed for sale. Spencer told the owners,

"If you paint the house, it will bring more money."
They said, "We don't want to do that, but if you want
to buy it from us, you can try painting it." Unable to
persuade them, he did buy it, paint it, and sell it at a
good profit. But he also made mistakes. He sold his
half interest in one piece of property only to see it
become many times more valuable when the
highway changed location.

In spite of the uncertainty of business, he said
he would rather run a peanut stand than work for
someone else again. He liked the flexibility of being his
own boss. He could visit people in the hospital or
attend a funeral or do other Church business without
asking someone's permission.

The first time a calendar salesman came he brought in
girlie calendars to show, but Spencer didn't want to
look. He said, "Don't you have something else?" The
salesman never brought that sort of calendar again.
When a farmer customer started to tell him a dirty
story, Spencer interrupted, saying that he had heard
that story before. And at a luncheon, when the person
came to the punch line of a vulgar story Spencer put a
big bite of food in his mouth, to make clear that
he was not participating.

Spencer and Camilla belonged to a square-dance club.
They also often had parties with a group of friends.
One New Year's Eve the party lasted until the sun came

up. About midnight they would call any friends they suspected might be sleeping to wish them a Happy New Year, sometimes long-distance—always collect. Every year Spencer called a friend who lived on the main road east of Safford. "Do you live on the highway to Solomonsville?" "Yes." "Well, you'd better get off because you're likely to be run over." Good-naturedly he fell for the same joke every year.

Spencer was playful, but not mean. Instead, people noted his kindness. One young woman had a blood disease that left her with blotched skin and stiff joints and clawlike hands. At dances Spencer always danced with her. He was not the only one, but he had a knack somehow of letting her forget her handicap.

The year 1933 brought both the depth of the Depression and personal disaster. Shortly before Eddie's third birthday he came in from play and complained of a sore throat. He vomited. In two days he had difficulty in standing up. They took him to a doctor, but the doctor could not figure out what was wrong. After more than two weeks of their wondering what was wrong, a chiropractor suggested poliomyelitis, a frequently crippling disease. They bundled the baby into their car and raced through the night without stopping, all the way to California. The specialist there recognized polio immediately and put Eddie in an isolation room in the hospital, where his parents could not be with him. The little boy screamed piteously until he practically lost his voice, not understanding why his parents had left him in a strange place, alone. Spencer and Camilla told him stories and sang him songs through the crack in the door, trying to quiet the frightened child.

Because it had already been so long since the disease started, he had to stay in isolation only a few days longer. Camilla stayed with him for many weeks, but Spencer had to go back to look after business and the rest of the family.

When he was little, Eddie was a mama's boy. A neighbor said, "How many times a day does that child say Mama? I tried to count them and it's thousands." Camilla splinted the legs that had been weakened and massaged them and exercised them. Spencer often carried Eddie on his shoulders, a progressively heavier load. It hurt his parents to hear their youngest son pray, "Bless me so that I can run and play and climb trees like the other children and fight!"

For years the family travelled to California each summer for Eddie to have another operation on his legs. It was vacation for the other children. One day LeVan, Olive Beth, and Andy went off to find a movie right after lunch. By mid-afternoon the parents started to worry. Later Spencer walked the streets and looked in the theaters and could not find them. Hours passed. At nine o'clock, sure it must be a kidnapping, Spencer went to notify the police. As he returned he found the three children just coming in. They had stayed to see the double feature three times. Little Andy had been ignored and came home with his pants soaked; that was the high point whenever the other children retold the family story of "the great kidnapping."

When the family travelled together they sang songs or played word games or guessed how far it was to a hill or building, then measured the distance. Spencer paid a dime each for memorizing the Articles of Faith or scriptures as they went along. Or the children could earn a nickel for brushing his hair.

Spencer was a tease with his family. He could read between the lines of the newspaper: "The Twenty-fourth of July parade in Safford Friday was attended by an estimated 2000 people (including handsome red-headed Eddie Kimball and his family)." Eddie would come running to see where he was mentioned in the newspaper. Or Spencer would remind Camilla about how a neighbor had named his cow after her or about the man who asked him if he was the fellow who married one of the "plain-faced Eyring girls." When he handed out the gifts under the Christmas tree he seemed to have a hard time seeing the one from Olive Beth's boy friend. They went to a movie regularly on a family ticket; Spencer would tell in great detail about the time the freckle-faced girl from Cactus Flat sat on Andrew's lap by mistake in the dark theater.

Though Eddie had difficulty in walking, the family treated him as normal and expected him to work and do chores. Spencer and Camilla set prices on things: ten cents for catching a mouse and twenty-five cents for trapping a gopher; five cents a day for practicing the piano, but paying the parents ten cents for every day the child didn't practice. The children earned money working in the yard or milking the cows or selling magazines or chopping weeds or picking cotton.

Spencer followed his father's example and reused old wire and straightened bent nails. One time he sent Andy and Eddie to tear down a shed and save the old lumber. As they took off the boards the shed collapsed on Eddie. Only the fact that he was standing in a doorway saved him from serious injury. Andy pulled him out and used his Boy Scout training to treat for shock.

Their parents expected the children to work and save, be involved in Church activities, take music lessons, do well in school, go on missions—to be successful in whatever they did. Spencer and Camilla attended programs or games in which the children participated. There was light discipline, lots of hugging, and high expectations. On their part the children usually responded as their parents hoped.

Olive Beth recalled just one occasion when her father spanked her. She was small and Spencer came home to find her walking around wearing two of his hats. It would have been all right if she had worn them on her head, but she wore them on her feet. Once Spencer gave Eddie a real scolding and the boy stomped off to his room, feeling unfairly treated and enjoying a sense of righteous anger. Then his father came in and apologized. Eddie burst into tears; it was impossible to stay mad at a father who could do that.

One night a teenage boy set their barn on fire. Spencer woke to a fire siren. With the fire department on the scene, Spencer took the time to wake Eddie up to see if he wanted to share the excitement. He asked the sleepy boy if he wanted to see the fire, but after peering drowsily out of the window Eddie went back to sleep while Spencer and Andy went out to help fight the fire.

Religion was important in the home, but there was no high pressure. The parents showed their deep commitment more by what they did than by what they said. In religious discussions Camilla was quick to admit there were many things she did not understand. Those were things she put on a mental shelf. At a later time she would take the questions down again. She found then that some of them had answers, others no longer seemed worth worrying about, and still others remained unanswered and were put back on the shelf for another time.

Spencer and Camilla valued friends and wanted their children to develop friendships too. One time when Spencer thought Eddie was spending too much time narrowly focused on school work, he said, "Son, I wouldn't mind if you got a few B's, if you were spending the time building friendships."

Spencer enjoyed his associations in the Rotary Club in Safford. He had joined in 1923 and he played the piano for meetings. The club raised money for youth camp and for free school lunches. After he had served a term as the Safford club president, Spencer's friends persuaded him to run for the position of district governor of all the clubs in Arizona. It would not be easy, because the Safford Club was a small one and also many Rotarians thought of Mormons as stuffy and self-righteous: "We don't smoke and we don't drink, thank you!" But Spencer didn't lecture or put on a long face. He had the ability to make friends with anyone; one man said, "Spencer can have more fun sober than most of us can drunk."

After campaigning for the office all year, Spencer arrived at the 1935 convention only to learn that the club president who managed the campaign for Harold Smith, his main opponent, had just died of a heart attack while playing golf. Spencer and his supporters decided it would be unfortunate to continue the campaign under the circumstances. So when the convention began, Spencer himself stood up and nominated the other candidate, Harold Smith, to be district governor. People swarmed about, congratulating him on his dramatic generous gesture, saying it was the finest example they had ever seen of the fellowship for which Rotary stood. As a result of his conceding the election, the next year no one even ran against him.

The international president of Rotary told the assembled district governors that year, "You naturally feel good when you visit a club and the men all stand and applaud you. But it is not *you* they are applauding, it is your position. If you doubt me, just go back again

next year, when you're no longer district governor."
Later, when Spencer received special treatment as a
Church leader, he remembered that.

During his year as district governor Spencer's service
had been so exceptional that the clubs voted to pay his
way to the international convention in France.
Spencer and Camilla drew on their savings for
Camilla's ticket and set off on a great adventure, an
eleven-week trip to Europe. No one whom they knew
had ever been to Europe, except on a mission. Because
Spencer was forty-two and a small-town businessman,
they never expected to see so much of the world again.
So when they got to Europe they packed every day
from early to late with seeing every museum,
monument, and castle.

At the gigantic convention banquet in Nice, France,
seven goblets of wine were set for each of them, but
Spencer was not even tempted to try them. As a
teenager he had already made that decision. He was
glad he did not have to make it over and over again.

Spencer had been stake clerk before his call as a
counselor in 1924, and at President Payne's
request he continued "temporarily" as stake clerk
for three years. When two successive clerks were
released after relatively short service, Spencer again
resumed double service as counselor and clerk. Finally

the other counselor suggested to Spencer that maybe it would be easier to get another good counselor than another good clerk. When in 1935 Elder Ballard, the Apostle, visited the stake and learned that Spencer had both jobs, he said he should have only one. Elder Ballard asked Spencer which position he preferred. Spencer first said, "I'll be glad to serve wherever you wish." When pressed, he said he thought he could best serve as clerk, since filling that position had been a problem. He was not concerned about status.

But since the stake clerk received a small salary, one of Spencer's friends wrote him, "Spencer, I'm disappointed in you. To think that you'd accept the money calling instead of the spiritual calling!" She predicted that within six months Spencer would apostatize.

Three years later Elder Ballard returned to divide the St. Joseph Stake, creating the new Mount Graham Stake and making Spencer its president. Spencer told Elder Ballard that perhaps he should not be called as stake president because there was a neighbor with whom he had had a serious disagreement about water rights. The Apostle lightly responded, "You can take care of that." So immediately after he became stake president Spencer went to the neighbor and tried to make amends. Both still thought they were right, but they were willing to put the dispute behind them; and Spencer later called the man to be a high councilor.

The Mount Graham Stake was huge, going from southeastern Arizona across southern New Mexico, clear to El Paso, Texas. To visit the farthest ward in the stake and return required a five-hundred-mile trip.

Being stake president involved conducting Church business and also helping people. For example, Spencer stood by a young man while his leg was amputated on a kitchen table. Sometimes transient workers would be referred to him for a wedding, and of course he did not charge anything. But when a man insisted on paying, Spencer said teasingly, "How much is she worth to you?" Knowing that was an unfair question, Spencer asked for five dollars and then gave it to the bride as a wedding present.

Once, invited to speak at a funeral, he got a real shock. The man whose funeral he thought it was came in and sat on the front row. It turned out that the funeral was for the man's brother.

In 1941 a terrific downpour pushed the Gila River out of its banks and flooded the town of Duncan. Houses made of mud bricks melted; frame houses shifted on their foundations. Hundreds of people were homeless. Spencer helped transport relief supplies from the Church welfare storehouse in Safford to the flood victims, primarily to Church members but also to others. He waded through swift water to survey the damage. Whole farms had almost disappeared, the fields gullied or covered with gravel. Crops in the fields had been swept away; a thousand sacks of onions floated downstream. After the emergency ended, Spencer coordinated the short-term clean-up of shoveling muck out of homes and a long-term program of rehabilitating farms with heavy equipment. This experience proved the ability of the Church welfare program, then only a few years old, to give substantial assistance in case of a major local disaster.

Spencer's business and Church and community involvements kept him working long hours and he sometimes felt as if he would explode, but these were the sorts of commitments he felt he could not turn away, and his strength as an organizer and his way with people made him constantly in demand.

Spencer had a chance to buy some property for business development in Las Vegas, Nevada, at a good price. He and Camilla discussed it for a long time and decided against getting involved in a gambling town, even though there was money to be made. Within a few months Las Vegas enjoyed a war-time boom. Spencer later said, "It is good we didn't buy that property. We would have been multimillionaires for sure, and I don't think I could have stood being rich." He once asked his nephew about business, "Are you making money?" When the answer was yes, he said, "I hope you don't make too much money."

On their twenty-fifth wedding anniversary Spencer and Camilla sent out six hundred invitations to friends to come to their home to help celebrate with food and visiting. They staggered the times people were invited so that not everyone would come at once. But the friends invited to come early just stayed, and the home got more and more packed until people could not even move around. Everyone had a wonderful time. Life seemed good to Spencer and Camilla as they settled into comfortable middle age.

Some months later, on July 8, 1943, Spencer arrived home for lunch as the phone rang. His son handed him the phone, saying, "Dad, it's Salt Lake calling." Through Spencer's mind flashed the thought that he was about to be called to a high position in the Church, but as he walked to the telephone he pushed the impulse aside as impossible— he was incapable of filling such a position. He heard the voice of President J. Reuben Clark, Jr., say, "Spencer, do you have a chair handy? The Brethren have just chosen you to fill one of the vacancies in the Quorum of the Twelve Apostles." Spencer protested that it couldn't be, that there must be a mistake, as he slid to the floor. President Clark reassured him. There was a long silence as Spencer thought about every petty thing he had done, the misunderstandings, the hurt feelings. It seemed that voices said, "How could *you* be an Apostle? You are not worthy. You can't do it."

President Clark finally interrupted the silence, "Are you there?" Spencer said of course he could give only one answer, but still he grasped for time. He would soon be in Colorado, visiting his son. Wouldn't it be a good idea if he were to come to Salt Lake City to talk about the call? President Clark agreed.

Unsteadily Spencer explained to Camilla and Andy and Eddie, who had listened wonderingly to his half of the conversation, what had been said. After a silent lunch he lay on the floor to rest, but his mind raced. Just when it promised rich rewards, he would be giving up a business he had struggled for twenty-five years to build; he would be uprooting his family, leaving behind life-long friends; he would be assuming responsibilities he felt incompetent to fulfill.
But he had long ago made a commitment to respond to any call from the Lord.

He started to weep; then he sobbed and could not stop. As he expressed his fears, Camilla stroked his hair, trying to comfort him. "You *can* do it," she reassured him. "You can do anything the Lord asks of you."

That night he did not sleep. And for a week he slept only fitfully, tossing in his bed.

He and Camilla arrived in Colorado to visit LeVan and his family, on the way to Salt Lake City. Early in the morning Spencer slipped out of the house, fasting, and started hiking up the nearby mountains, straight up without a path. He nearly stepped on a rattlesnake and jumped as it struck at him; he wondered if that were an omen. He wept as he climbed ever higher, alternately praying for confirmation from the Lord and criticizing himself for his weaknesses. He knew there were possible human explanations why he had been called—his being a cousin to President Clark, his father's friendship with President Grant, his being an effective stake president, his work on the Duncan flood—but he also believed in the inspiration of Church leaders. *Someone* had to be called; was it really the Lord's will that *he* be the one?

He had climbed a long way, but he felt impelled to climb on up the rough rocks to the top of a cliff. He looked at the valley spread below him and the thought

crossed his mind that it would be easy to end his struggle by just flinging himself from the height. He prayed as he never had prayed before, not for a vision but for some sort of answer. For a long time he wept and struggled. And finally his answer came. As in a dream he sensed his grandfather and the great apostolic work he had done. And with the experience came a calm like the dying wind, the quieting wave after the storm is past. His tears dried, his soul was at peace. A great burden had been lifted and he felt nearer the Lord than ever before in his life.

In Salt Lake City he met with David O. McKay, counselor in the First Presidency, who reaffirmed the call and notified the radio stations and newspapers of the appointment. When Spencer returned to Arizona to sell his business and move his family to Utah, he had a hard time getting any work done. Friends all wanted to congratulate him.

Orville Allen told Spencer of a time when Spencer was just a boy and Orville was helping Spencer's father unload some pumpkins for pig feed. They heard Spencer singing at his milking, and Andrew said, "That Spencer is a good boy. I have dedicated him to the Lord, and someday he will become a mighty man in the Church."

Though some of Spencer's visitors exclaimed, like Orville, "It was inevitable that you be called," and others assured him, "I knew something like that was coming," Evans Coleman was the one who more nearly expressed what Spencer was feeling. "You know, Spencer, it is clear that the *Lord* called you— because no one else would have thought of you!"

Spencer went around to people he had done business with and said, "If you think I have ever taken unfair advantage of you, please tell me. I want to make it right with you." A couple thought they should have a little more money on some sales, and Spencer paid them what they asked, but all the rest just waved his offer aside. He talked again with the neighbor with whom he had had an old water dispute, and even took flowers. He wanted no bad feelings when he left.

Spencer and Camilla gave some things away, packed up the rest, and moved to Utah. The two sons at home felt imposed upon and complained about leaving Arizona. While travelling to Utah, Spencer explained something about loyalty. "We have loved Arizona and we'll never forget her, but from now on Utah is our home, and while we live there Utah has the finest climate, the most beautiful scenery, and the best people in the world."

After moving the family, Spencer returned again to Arizona to finish up his responsibilities. On Sunday he attended testimony meeting in three different wards and everyone who spoke praised him. He wrote to Camilla that, because of time constraints, "we went late to the last two meetings. I was the first corpse I had ever seen that had three funerals in one day and was late for two of them."

At October general conference 1943 the Church sustained Spencer W. Kimball and Ezra Taft Benson as Apostles. Various emotions crowded in—humility, gratitude, excitement, uncertainty. And when the invalid President Grant ordained them and admonished Spencer "to make this cause and this labor first and foremost in all your thoughts," Spencer fully committed himself to that goal. Spencer was forty-eight, starting a new life.

He needed to get accustomed to new responsibilities, and the Church had to get acquainted with a new General Authority. In one of his first stake conferences he was introduced as Ezra Taft Benson. "That's all right with me," he said to the congregation. "Just don't tell Brother Benson!" And after another meeting a man shook his hand. "I am glad you came, Brother Richards; I always used to get you mixed up with Brother Lee."

Soon after he joined the Quorum of the Twelve one of the Apostles had to be excommunicated for personal misconduct. Having to do that shook the quorum members. Many of them wept in sorrow. The painful experience reminded Spencer that no mortal—not even an Apostle—is beyond temptation, and that everyone, however high his position, stands accountable for his conduct.

Several times as an Apostle Spencer had near accidents that left him feeling that the Lord looked after him. On his first mission tour the car skidded in the snow and very nearly ended up in a deep gully. On that tour he travelled 4,500 miles by car in seventeen days and spoke at more than forty meetings. He worked hard and determinedly. In Wyoming a public official advised them not to try to get to Rawlings through snowdrifts, but Spencer knew people would be waiting. He and the mission president got an ax, firewood, extra blankets, and started off. They had to take a long detour to avoid roads that were drifted closed, but they got to Rawlings.

During one four-month period he slept in his own bed only two nights. The strain of constant travel was aggravated by the boils he suffered over a period of years, often several at a time, great red swellings excruciatingly painful to the slightest touch. They gave him intense discomfort but he kept on going, never excusing himself just because he was in pain.

He met thousands of people and often amazed them with his recall of their names. A young woman spoke to him at a stake conference. "I thought maybe you would remember me because I am Blanche's sister." He responded, "No, I remember you because you are Julia." Another time R. H. Daines, a stake leader in New Jersey whom Spencer had met, telephoned his friend Henry Eyring in Utah. Spencer happened to be at the Eyring home (Henry was Spencer's brother-in-law) and answered the telephone. In response to a request to speak to Henry, Spencer said, "I'm sorry, he is not here right now. Is this by any chance Brother Daines?"

Spencer was travelling, visiting the Eastern States Mission, when President Heber J. Grant died in 1945. Spencer hurried back to Salt Lake City to participate in the funeral and in the naming of a new President. Some people thought that the senior Apostle, George Albert Smith, was too old at seventy-five to assume responsibility for the Church; they urged that if the senior Apostle were routinely named, that would guarantee that the President would nearly always be an old man. But the quorum rejected that concept and felt impressed unanimously to name George Albert Smith President.

Though much of his administrative work in the Church depended on his own efforts, as had success in business, he often felt divine guidance, particularly in choosing new leaders from men he had inverviewed only briefly. He might struggle with the choice until a certain man would walk into the room. He and Elder Hugh B. Brown once interviewed more than twenty-five leaders during a Saturday and to that point had had no feeling that they had met the right person for the stake president's position. Two other men suggested as possibilities were then out of town but returned Saturday night. When the second man came in, just thirty-three years old and new in the community, both General Authorities felt immediately that this was the man. On another occasion a new stake president expressed no surprise when called. When Spencer asked why, the man explained that two days earlier words had formed in his mind, as though from a voice, saying simply, "You will be the president of the new stake."

One day two young returned missionaries from Mexico, who were enrolled at BYU, had just a frozen carton of chocolate milk to last them the next several days. Answering a knock at the door they found Spencer standing there. He had met them six months before in Mexico and recently their former mission president had mentioned they were at BYU. He had tracked them down. Now he offered his good wishes and, in saying goodbye, pressed a twenty-dollar bill into one's hand. One said, "How did he know?" The other replied, "Because he is a prophet."

While Spencer was meeting with a group of missionaries a man came requesting a blessing for his long-useless right arm, which was in a cast straight out from his body. Spencer interrupted the meeting to administer to him. A few hours later the man was back, waving his arm delightedly. He explained that when he sat down to eat dinner with his left hand he asked himself, "Where is my faith?" He got a hammer and broke off the cast and began successfully using his right arm.

A child's esophagus had been badly burned with lye and nearly closed with scar tissue. The doctor had told the parents that a four-hour operation offered the child's only chance at survival. But within hours after receiving a blessing from Elder Kimball the baby started eating soft food with a good appetite.

He listened to the Spirit, not always giving precisely the blessing asked for. Spencer visited a badly burned woman in the hospital who begged to be allowed to die. Spencer blessed her instead to live and rear her children.

He usually asked the Lord for a blessing "if it be Thy will," but sometimes he made unconditional promises in the name of the Lord. He trembled afterward from the responsibility he had assumed, but he felt he had to say what the Spirit impelled.

Elder Kimball stressed that it was not always the Lord's will that the sick be healed. In some cases he offered comfort rather than recovery. A young father lay suffering with cancer and the Apostle blessed him with relative freedom from pain, and peace in the knowledge that his family would be well cared for. He died three months later, having suffered little.

On another type of errand one time he was sent to a rural ward torn apart by bitterness, with people accusing one another. At seven in the evening he met with the people involved. For hours the meeting continued, the people cold and angry. After listening, Spencer told them he thought both sides had some guilt and that they all needed to forgive. He said that if they could not forgive one another, the right to have the sacrament might be taken away, or the ward might have to be dissolved. Even that was not enough to move them. It got to be well after midnight. Finally he preached from the scriptures, with great power, that those who refuse to forgive are guilty of even greater sin than those who have caused offense. And that broke the logjam. At two o'clock in the morning the meeting ended in tears of forgiveness.

Interviewing a prospective missionary who stated he had been chaste, Spencer felt a sense of depression and uneasiness. He asked more pointed questions, but the young man insisted he had never done anything wrong. Spencer put the mission papers on his desk and excused the man, saying, "I will need to see you later." Some hours later the young man returned, in tears, confessing and saying, "You knew I lied."

He didn't like to be waited on. One time his host insisted on shining Spencer's shoes. After giving the shoes a good polish the man said, "There! Finished!" But Spencer replied, "Oh, no, not yet! Now you sit here and I'll shine yours!"

General Authorities stayed in stake leaders' homes when visiting stake conferences nearly every week. He would play the piano for the children, singing Primary songs with them—"They'll forget my sermons, but they'll never forget our singing." And he was quick to help with the chores. In Rigby he insisted on milking two cows at the stake president's farm. Next morning he was up early and helped again. At the conference the president mentioned his help, and after the meeting people came up to say, "Next time we hope you'll stay with us." After Bishop Marvin O. Ashton attended the next Rigby conference he approached Spencer in mock anger. "As I drove up to the stake president's farm, there on the gate hung overalls and a milk bucket for me. When I asked what that was all about, they said, 'Well, Brother Kimball helped with the milking.'"

Being a General Authority demanded his serious
effort, but Spencer managed to keep a sense of humor.
For a General Authority social he organized a quartet
and put on a skit about a miracle hair tonic. As they
sang, they doused the heads of two bald Church
leaders with hair tonic and placed a turban-like
towel on each head. When the towels were unwound
one head sported a shock of red hair and the other
a wig of long black curls.

Stories Spencer told were often on himself, such as the
time a group of Primary children came to visit him.
When the teacher asked her class if they knew who
this man was, there was silence. Finally one small boy
looked at the Apostle, straining to remember, and
answered, "I know I've seen that mug somewhere."

In 1946 President George Albert Smith called Spencer into his office for a special assignment "to look after the Indians in all the world." At that time only a handful of Indians belonged to the Church, and the new Navajo-Zuni Mission in Arizona and New Mexico had just been organized. Spencer thought back on his patriarchal blessing, which said in part, "You will preach the gospel to many people, but more especially to the Lamanites." This might be the fulfillment.

Just a few weeks after receiving the assignment, he woke in the night with a strange foreboding. He opened a book and tried to read, but he sensed something horrible in the room, like an enemy there to destroy him. He broke into a fearful sweat; he struggled against a bleak, dark unknown. Finally he remembered from the temple ceremony that he had the power to rebuke the evil spirit. After he did so, relief came and he was able to sleep. He woke next morning exhausted. As he mused about it he wondered whether his new assignment might be a special threat to Satan.

He began to travel on the reservations, meeting and teaching, blessing the sick, encouraging the missionary work. The missionaries could not rent, buy, or build on the reservations without permission, and ministers of other churches opposed any Mormon presence. President Smith himself went to a meeting on the Navajo Reservation to try to quiet their fears and plead for tolerance. But it took several years before the tribal council would let the Mormons do more than just visit the reservation.

Helping the Indians had many sides. In 1947 a harsh early winter left many Navajos close to starvation. Spencer stirred up interest in their trouble by writing newspaper and magazine articles, giving talks, contacting service clubs. The Church welfare system provided food and the *Deseret News* created an Indian Aid Caravan of trucks to take food and warm clothing to the Indians. A Red Cross official said of the incident that "one little man" had wakened the country and even motivated Congress to vote for money to help deal with the Indians' problems.

But Spencer saw the crisis as only a symptom of deeper troubles. The government had neglected its agreement to provide schools for the Indians. They needed better education and better roads in order to help solve their own problems.

During the same cold winter a seventeen-year-old Indian girl, Helen John, had been working in the snow in the sugar beet fields of Utah. She begged her employers to let her stay on their farm in a tent all winter so she could go to school there. Golden Buchanan of the stake presidency came to talk with her, and as he thought of her situation the concept came to him of having Indians stay with Latter-day

Saint families during the school year. He wrote to
Spencer and in a few days Spencer came to his home.
To their surprise Spencer asked the Buchanans
whether *they* would take Helen into their home that
school year as a daughter. That was a hard question,
because Sister Buchanan had grown up with a fear of
Indians, and the children thought their friends would
laugh, but after a night of thought and prayer the
family agreed. Helen didn't stay long the first time, but
she later returned bringing other Indian children with
her. Within a few years, under Spencer's
encouragement, the program grew until the Church
officially took it over. The Indian Student Placement
Program ultimately grew to nearly five thousand
children a year, before improved schools and roads on
the reservations decreased its importance.

Spencer's interest in Indians involved people as well as
programs. One Indian girl lived in his home for a while
and another lived with his daughter. He helped boys in
trouble with the law get a lawyer. He arranged
financial help for college students and missionaries.
He hugged the children.

Spencer performed the wedding for an Indian boy and
a white girl, even though her parents refused to attend
the temple ceremony. While he always warned
couples that their marriage might be more difficult
because of their different backgrounds, there was
nothing else wrong with marriage between red and

white. Once the young couple had made their decision, he considered the parents had made a sad mistake in rejecting their daughter.

He used his talks at general conference and at BYU to explain the responsibility others had to accept and help those of another race who had a great destiny promised by the scriptures. "The only difference between them and us," he said, "is opportunity. They are equal to us in their mental powers. Racial prejudice is of the devil and of ignorance."

I n 1948, visiting the reservations, the car in which Spencer and mission president Golden Buchanan rode stuck fast in deep sand. They pushed and strained to free it. Spencer's heart could not take this additional stress. That night he lay on the bedroom floor in agonizing pain. But the worst passed and he continued the mission tour, saying nothing until he returned to Salt Lake many days later. Even though his doctor insisted he should discontinue his work for a month, Spencer ignored that advice and soon felt crushing pain again, which finally persuaded him that he had no choice. Seven weeks of house confinement drove him into depression for occupying a place in the quorum without being able to help with its work. This mood alternated with a fierce determination to get well.

Golden Buchanan drove him to the Navajo Reservation, where he camped near the home of Howela and Ruth Polacca, resting, studying, walking, learning a Navajo song from little Francis Polacca, carving a crude life-size self-portrait from white stone.

After two weeks he felt well, but the return to work caused a new heart attack and he had to spend another six weeks in California, away from well-meaning visitors and ringing phones. With time for study he got a twenty-five-foot roll of shelf paper and plotted out two time lines: one for the religious and the other for the secular history of the world. He also wrote long letters to family members, encouraging their activity in the Church.

His brother had once said, "Spencer, you can't keep burning the candle at both ends." His response had been, "I have to, because the other Church leaders are so much better prepared than I am." That feeling of inadequacy had induced him to work doubly hard, which had in turn cost him precious time recovering from illness, but he seemed incapable of going at less than full speed. As soon as the First Presidency permitted, he plunged back into work, saying nothing about his new pains.

He had a dream about going to the family of a dead friend, who had not been much interested in religion.

In his dream the family paid little attention to him, but the man stood by, unseen, more handsome than in life, looking pleased at Spencer's efforts. Though Spencer did not relish going to the inactive family, he felt impelled to do so. On his next trip to Arizona he met with them. They only listened politely, but he felt he had fulfilled a responsibility.

On that same trip Spencer invited a friend who seemed spiritually adrift to go camping with him. "I'll get the food," the friend said. "I thought maybe we would go fasting," said Spencer, "so we won't need any food." They camped out from Saturday to Monday at a meadow in the high mountains, reading the scriptures, praying, and talking. On Monday, when they prepared to leave, the car wouldn't start. They worked at it for some time, with no results. Then they prayed about their problem and after only a moment more of tinkering the car started up.

In 1950 persistent hoarseness sent Spencer to a cancer specialist. A white spot on his vocal cord called for biopsy. At the hospital the doctor put him under general anesthetic, put a tube down his throat, and snipped out some tissue from his vocal cord for examination. After the operation an orderly began to wheel Spencer back to his hospital room. Angry at something, the man swore, using the Lord's name. Only half-conscious, Spencer pleaded weakly, "Please don't say that. I love him more than anything in this world. Please." The orderly apologized.

The doctor found no cancer but prescribed burning the infected spot. Instead Spencer had a priesthood administration, and within a few days he had recovered his voice. After worrying about how loss of his voice would limit his ministry, he rejoiced at being able to sing again.

President George Albert Smith died in 1951 and the Quorum of the Twelve met to choose his successor. As David O. McKay was speaking, Spencer saw him in his majesty and power. "I saw him as the President of the Church. . . . There was no doubt in my mind. It was a soul-satisfying feeling. It was hardly a light—it was more like a sudden flood of warmth and into my mind came the thought: 'A PROPHET'S MANTLE.' "

Spencer wrote in his journal: "No man will live long enough to become President of this Church ever who is not the proper one to give it leadership. Each leader in his own peculiar way has made a great contribution to the onward march of the Church. No one of the nine Presidents had all the virtues nor all the abilities. Each in his own way and time filled a special need and made his great contribution. This I know. This I know."

Under the leadership of a new President, Spencer continued his work—travelling, teaching, counseling. He always felt he was not good enough for his calling, but he never quit. He often joked about being small. The joking covered insecurity; his shortness bothered him. He wrote home, "Yesterday as we got in the elevator to come down, two little midgets came down with us. I certainly got a lift when I could look far down on grown men. . . . I frequently find men thinner, but seldom find them shorter."

His being gone so often on Church business, and so preoccupied even when at home, left Camilla sometimes feeling neglected. She wrote him, "Anyone who thinks being the wife of one of the General Authorities is a bed of roses should try it once, shouldn't they? . . . I wouldn't have you be one whit less valiant in the pursuit of your duty. . . , but it is comforting to be reassured once in a while that you realize I am standing by. . . ."

He carried on a huge correspondence. He usually wrote individual letters to the families of the missionaries he met. One Christmas a group of fifty Indian children each sent him a letter. He responded with fifty long individual letters.

His concern was more for others than for himself. Camilla once received flowers with a note, saying that Spencer had gone out of his way to help someone on crutches. "Since he is the type of man who would appreciate a gift to you more than to himself, it pleases me to send you these roses." No signature.

One blizzardy night Spencer was stranded with a car that would not start. He tried repeatedly to telephone for help and finally reached a service station owner who would come. The man worked in the bitter cold, taking the battery out, then took Spencer with him to his station where it was warm and tried to recharge the battery, but found it had to be replaced. "You're in luck," he said. "I have a battery in stock that will fit. It usually costs $18, but it's on sale right now for $15." Spencer said, "I'd like to buy the battery, but I want to pay $18." "You don't understand, sir; it is on sale." "I do understand, but you've already gone out of your way to help me. I want to pay full price." "Well, sir, I can put your old battery back in, just like it was, and your car still won't run, but if you want to buy this battery the price is $15." Spencer finally agreed, but he showed his gratitude by trading faithfully at that service station as long as the owner stayed in business. Spencer went out of his way to bring other customers to trade there, too.

In 1955 President McKay asked Spencer to visit all the missions in Europe, a task that took nearly six months. He and Camilla had been to Europe as tourists in 1937, but since then World War II, the greatest war the world had known, had devastated most of the major cities. Ten years after the end of the war, the bomb-ruined cities and the Nazi death-camps they visited showed the cruelty of intolerance and war. In thirteen countries Spencer preached the gospel of peace and encouraged Church members to build the Church where they were. The temple in Switzerland, just completed, gave the Church members in Europe access to all the blessings they could have anywhere in the world. He told them that in spite of their poverty they could find a way to go to the temple. If they knew how important the temple ordinances were, they would be willing to walk to Switzerland.

That long, difficult assignment over, he returned to the usual stake conference visits, administrative work, and counseling. Some days brought complicated problems. He received a call from a woman in California that her husband, in a seedy Salt Lake hotel, needed help. He arranged for the man to come to his office, but when he did not come, Spencer went to the hotel, suffering intense pain from a bad back all the while. Finding the man staggering drunk, Spencer asked him to give up his bottle. First he denied having a bottle, but finally gave it to Spencer to pour the contents down the drain. Spencer then bathed the man in cold water and sobered him up enough to go to Alcoholics Anonymous. While Spencer checked him out of the hotel the man disappeared. Spencer looked everywhere for him. Finally he left the man's bags at AA and caught a train for a conference appointment.

On his return he found the man had taken treatment and was better. Two years later nearly the same story played over again. And for years he kept getting calls for help and requests for loans from the man. Spencer never gave up as long as the man would keep trying.

He had a number of such "problem boys." President Clark once scolded Spencer for spending too much of his time counseling with people "who don't have all their buttons," but Spencer couldn't choose among those who needed his help.

Because it is easier to be good when someone is watching, a better measure of character is what one does when he thinks no one is noticing. A pregnant young mother, threatening miscarriage of an unborn baby, found herself stranded in an airport by a snowstorm. She stood in line trying to get on another airplane, and she pushed her wet, crying child along the floor because she had instructions to lift the child as little as possible. An older man offered help. He held the child and talked the people in line into letting her move to the head of the line. She was able to get a reservation, and he helped her settle down to wait. Then he left. Some weeks later she saw a picture of Spencer Kimball and recognized him as the stranger who had helped her.

December 1956. As Spencer and Camilla travelled to a stake conference in Arizona, their car skidded off the icy road and careened down the mountainside. When the car stopped Spencer found he was only shaken up. He said, "Well, Mama, I guess we are all right," but Camilla groaned in pain, "No, I am dying." With help he managed to bend the fender away from the tire and get the car onto the highway down below. They struggled thirty-five miles back to a hospital, where an x-ray showed that Camilla suffered broken ribs and a punctured lung but no permanent injury. Spencer blamed himself because he had had a strong feeling to go the longer route, around the mountain, but had disregarded the feeling because the roads looked good. He had had a number of near accidents over the years and wondered whether the devil wanted his destruction; he firmly believed the Lord looked out for his safety.

Spencer's throat began to bother him again, nearly seven years since his healing. His voice was weakening and his throat bled some. He went calmly to New York to consult the foremost specialist in the world on throat cancer. Cancer had been Spencer's special fear ever since he watched his sister die a horrible death from cancer of the face. But he had reconciled himself: his family were all married and settled, and he had been able to give thirteen years of service in the apostleship. As he thought back on a recent vivid dream in which his father had come to him, smiling radiantly, his fear of death melted away. He felt himself in the Lord's hands.

A biopsy proved inconclusive and he received orders to maintain complete silence for a month while the vocal cord healed from the cutting. That was hard. People reacted in various ways. Most who saw that he could not speak assumed he was also deaf and shouted in his ear or replied to his notes by writing or by some sort of sign language. At a dinner a friend said, "Well, I see that at least you can eat." A little grandson, seeing him silent, talked to him in a whisper, as though they were sharing a secret.

The throat would not heal and Spencer returned to New York. This time the surgeon was sure it was cancer and saw no solution but to remove the whole voice box. Spencer and Harold B. Lee, explaining how important Spencer's voice was to his ministry, asked if less radical surgery might do. The doctor thought they were foolish, but agreed to take only one vocal cord and half of the other, preserving the chance of a little voice.

Awaiting the operation, Spencer spent what voice he had left, talking on the telephone for what might be the last time, even singing a few notes, talking, talking compulsively. He accepted the decision in his mind, but he struggled in spirit until Elder Lee administered to him.

When he woke up he had a four-inch long cut in his neck and a tube sticking out of it for him to breathe through. A nurse brought him pills and he took them. She brought more and he took those. She brought a third set and he asked, voicelessly, "What am I taking?" She would not tell him; she just said, "You've got to take them." He said, "Just put them down." She did not know how stubborn her patient was or how reluctant he was to take unneeded drugs. He never took the pills.

The incision became infected and dreadfully painful. It took weeks to heal. "Insomnia is my trouble," he wrote his children. "I can't sleep. Why, I couldn't even doze in sacrament meeting yesterday."

He did not have a real voice any more, just a weak rasp, but he determined to make the most of it. He could manage conversation, but he feared public speaking. Several months later he attended, in the Gila Valley, a stake conference being conducted by Elder Delbert L. Stapley. When Elder Stapley asked Spencer to speak he was tempted to decline, but then he decided he would never have a more understanding audience for his first effort. He explained to his friends, "I went away to the East and fell among cutthroats and thieves. They slit my throat and stole my voice." The people laughed, and he was grateful to be back at his work again.

At the next general conference he found that people would listen to him; indeed, people paid special attention because of his unusual voice. President Clark asked him about a painful boil on his neck; Spencer replied, "I am so glad to be able to speak that I can't be bothered by anything as minor as a boil."

In 1959 Spencer visited the three missions in South America. He warned missionaries working in branches that they should not do anything that members could do for themselves. If a member could play only one hymn on the piano, they should sing that one until he learned another.

In Brazil, particularly, he confronted the problem of race. He was pleased that everyone seemed happy with a black woman as Relief Society president in one branch. And he suffered with a man who had only a small percentage of black ancestry but under Church policy at that time could not hold the priesthood. Spencer pointed out to him that there were many important things he still could do in the Church.

People were always his first concern. As he visited one stake a bishop asked if he could find time to visit the hospital to bless a dying man. Between meetings Spencer said, "Let's go!" The bishop drove him at breakneck speed to the hospital, they ran across the parking lot, up the stairs and down the hall. Then, as they entered the man's room, "there was an amazing change. Elder Kimball seemed to have all the time in the world." After they visited with the man, gave him a blessing, and took an unhurried leave, they ran back to the car and raced to the conference, arriving just a few minutes late for the afternoon meeting.

Assigned to organize new stakes in Australia and New Zealand, Spencer also had to participate in the excommunication of several missionaries who had become involved in immorality. He mourned especially because other missionaries might have been able to prevent the tragedy if they had been willing to warn the mission president that their fellow missionaries were starting to break mission rules.

Spencer and Camilla returned home from Australia by going on around the world. They stopped in India to talk with a young minister who had become converted to the Church through a spiritual manifestation after reading Church literature. Spencer did not encourage him, knowing he would probably lose his friends and family and job, and he would not have any Church organization in India to offer support. But when Mangal Dan Dipty insisted he was willing to take the consequences, Spencer felt he could not refuse to baptize him. They went to a muddy river and the Apostle baptized the determined young man, confirmed him, and reluctantly left him to face his future alone. Later, after Brother Dipty did suffer rejection, Spencer and others were able to help him emigrate to Canada and then the United States.

On the way from India the Kimballs went to the Holy Land. They liked it so much that at Christmastime they returned to Bethlehem, wanting to experience Christmas there. They found the city crowded and noisy, with carols blaring over loudspeakers. Two rival shrines each claimed to be the actual birthplace of Christ, competing for tourists. They escaped from the hubbub and went out to the hillsides opposite Bethlehem, where the shepherds might have watched their flocks by night. In that quiet place they sang and prayed and recaptured for themselves some of the wonder of the Advent.

Their assignment took them from Israel to East Berlin. They felt the same oppressive feeling they had experienced there six years earlier. They tried to get to the meeting place without being followed. About eighty members met in a small hall—a faithful handful. Spencer felt that he was among great and noble souls. Because his notes of the meetings included leaders' names and he feared they might be arrested by the secret police, he hid his notes between the car's seat cushions as he left. The border guards who searched the car did not find his notes.

In 1965 Spencer received the assignment to supervise the missions in South America. This meant sometimes travelling long distances over poor roads. Once for three nights straight Spencer and Camilla slept sitting up in the mission car as they were driven long distances to meet their schedule. When a mechanic looked at the car after the tour ended he expressed disbelief that the car could be running at all with the generator brushes completely worn off.

Wherever he went people sang "We Thank Thee, O God, for a Prophet." But he knew that when they sang and when they showered him with flower petals they did it only because he served as a symbol of something greater.

Spencer tried to teach equality and humility by taking off his coat and shoveling sand at a chapel construction site in Montevideo. And for a conference session in the unfinished building the next day he helped set up the chairs. One mission president told a friend, "Trying to keep up with him is killing me."

They travelled over nearly impassable roads to back country so rugged that the missionaries there dressed in Levi's and boots. During a missionary meeting Spencer saw two men standing outside, waiting. After the meeting they humbly handed him a basket containing a dozen small eggs. No gift had ever touched him more.

Spencer explained to President McKay that so far missionaries in South America had gone almost exclusively to people of European descent, while there were millions of pure-blood Indians who spoke no Spanish in the high valleys of the Andes Mountains. With the President's permission he expanded missionary work to the Indians in their own languages.

He joined with the missionaries in the Indian village of Peguchi and preached in a little hollow where paths came together. A group of Indians gathered to listen to him speak as the mission president interpreted. Spencer talked of the visit of Christ to their ancestors. And as he pointed to the sky, from which Christ had descended, every eye followed his gesture, as if to see the Lord. He saw a promise of success in their openness and enthusiasm.

During this time riots in United States' cities dominated the news. And the civil rights movement brought criticism to the Church for its refusal to confer the priesthood on black men. The Vietnam war involved more and more soldiers from the United States, and the military draft took young men who might have served missions. It was a troubled time.

After four years supervising the South American missions, Spencer received assignment to supervise the missions in Britain. He approached this task with the same zeal. He found that unfortunately missionaries had baptized a great many young people without their really understanding the meaning of baptism. All these members who had no real interest made it very difficult to be a leader. To the extent that efforts to find and activate these people failed, the Church finally authorized their removal from the membership lists.

Wherever he went, in Britain or elsewhere, at conferences Spencer called up twelve-year-old boys and asked them what they would be doing at nineteen. Whether they knew the answer or not he would give them a dollar or its equivalent for their missionary fund. One little boy said he planned to be a doctor; Spencer said, "You'll be a better doctor after you have been on a mission," and gave him a dollar. The boy's parents later sent Spencer ten dollars to use for other boys. A friend gave him a whole box of silver dollars, labeled "Seeds for the Spencer W. Kimball Missionary Garden." Sometimes he would give dollars to girls, for them to start a fund for travel to the temple for their wedding.

In 1969 Spencer published *The Miracle of Forgiveness*, a book about the process of repentance. It grew out of his twenty-five years of counseling people in trouble and reflected his hope that they could straighten out their lives. He had spent ten years, off and on, writing it. There were few sins or troubles he had not helped people wrestle with. It seemed to him that as time went on more and more people had hardened their hearts and weren't even trying to live righteously.

Once a couple came to him complaining that, even though they had been immoral, it was just once, and their bishop had had the nerve to refuse them a recommend to be married in the temple. While they sat there he telephoned the bishop and asked him if what they said was true. Then he said, "Bishop, you did just right. Now I think you should consider excommunicating them both for their unrepentant attitude. They are looking for someone else to blame for their inconvenience instead of being sorrowful for their sin." After he hung up, the startled couple quickly reconsidered their position.

But generally he was as gentle with individual sinners as he was publicly critical of sin. A woman came to him in the temple once and asked, "Brother Kimball, do you remember me?" He thought hard. Embarrassed, he said, "I'm sorry, I don't." She seemed greatly relieved and said, "You spent hours with me and my husband some years ago, long into the night. Perhaps if you do not remember me or my sins, the Lord can also forget them." She pressed his hand gratefully.

In 1970 David O. McKay died after nineteen years as President of the Church. In those years the Church had grown from 180 stakes to 500, and two-thirds of the members had known no other President. At ninety-three, Joseph Fielding Smith, the senior Apostle, succeeded President McKay.

At about that time Spencer's throat cancer came back. It had been thirteen years since the removal of most of his vocal cords, and the surgeon who had operated before insisted now that removal of the whole voice box offered the best solution. While Spencer was considering what to do, he got a second shock. He discovered that his increasing weariness resulted from a heart that was about to fail at any moment. He needed a heart operation immediately, but that made no sense unless his cancer were taken care of first. Even though the cancer surgeon had low regard for radiation treatment, Spencer decided to try it, because it left at least a chance of preserving what voice he had. After twenty-four cobalt treatments the cancer was stopped.

Dr. Russell Nelson then operated on his heart, putting in a mechanical valve and repairing clogged arteries. Dr. Nelson said later that in the thousands of steps in the complicated operation, not one tiny thing had gone wrong. It went perfectly. And at the end of the operation he had been impressed that the man whose life he had just saved would preside over the Church.

While Spencer was still recovering, President Smith died and Harold B. Lee replaced him. Spencer had sat next to Elder Lee in the quorum through nearly thirty years. There was great love between them. President Lee was younger and in better health than Spencer, so there seemed no real possibility of Spencer's succeeding to the Presidency. And for that he and Camilla expressed gratitude every day, not wanting the awesome burden that the President had to carry.

But the day after Christmas 1973 President Lee suffered a sudden attack while in the hospital for a check-up. Arthur Haycock, President Lee's secretary, immediately called the counselors and then called Spencer, as President of the quorum. "President Lee is very ill. I think you ought to come." Spencer left for the hospital on the run and arrived first.

When President Marion G. Romney, President Lee's counselor, arrived moments later Spencer asked, "What would you like me to do?" President Romney said, "There is nothing to do but pray and wait." While the doctors struggled to save President Lee's life, they prayed and waited.

When word came that President Lee had died, Marion Romney turned to Spencer, who was now the presiding officer of the Church, and asked, "President Kimball, what would you like me to do?"

Spencer felt overwhelmed by the new responsibility, inadequate but still willing to do his best. He knew that God would not have brought him to this position without a willingness to give him the guidance he needed. He recalled an occasion when he had complained to Harold B. Lee about his inadequacies and Elder Lee had said in a disappointed tone, "Spencer, be yourself. Use the talents the Lord has given you." That would have to do, but perhaps it would be enough. President Lee had once said to someone else, "Spencer is one of the tallest men I've ever known, from the shoulders up."

On Sunday, December 30, 1973, the Quorum of the Twelve, after seeking the inspiration of God, named Spencer Woolley Kimball the twelfth President of the Church. Spencer had been an Apostle for thirty years and was seventy-eight years old, with a history of major health problems. Many people thought his administration would be rather short, and that he would not have the energy to accomplish much. They foresaw just a "caretaker" period. One little boy, brought into his office to shake his hand, said frankly, "I wanted to see you before you died."

At President Lee's funeral Spencer said, "A giant redwood has fallen and left a great space in the forest." He had to fill that space. He knew he could not do it

A giant
redwood tree
has fallen and
left a great space
in the forest.

alone and he was not alone. He felt the Lord guided many of his decisions. One night he felt President Lee's spirit near, reassuring him. Another night, half sleeping, he saw his father.

He fretted about his first press conference, at which dozens of reporters and cameramen crowded around, because he knew one slip of the tongue could produce endless trouble. Now that he spoke as the prophet, people responded in a different way; everything he said and did took on special importance.

In April he talked to the Regional Representatives about missionary work. He used the same theme he had used before, that in the Church there was great unused capacity for spreading the gospel. He emphasized that the Lord would open doors to nations now closed to missionary work only when Church members were prepared to walk through them. This time the challenge "Are we prepared to lengthen our stride?" sounded as a trumpet. He spoke for more than an hour with a spiritual power that touched his audience. And he spoke as the prophet. After he spoke, President Benson responded, "President Kimball, in all the years these meetings have been held, we have never heard such an address as you have just given." The number of missionaries (already growing) climbed even more steeply.

After the last session of April conference,
at which the whole Church had sustained him
President, Spencer and Camilla opened their home to
friends and relatives to enjoy a buffet meal Camilla had
spent days preparing. Because of threats against
the Church and the new President, the city had posted
a patrol car outside as a precaution. During the
evening Spencer filled a plate with food, left his
guests, and slipped out almost unnoticed to take
it to the police officer on duty.

There had been little need for special security for the
Church President in the 1900s until demonstrations
against the Church by nonmembers and threats from
dissidents required full-time security. But safety cost
loss of privacy and loss of freedom.

During the trial of followers of Ervil LeBaron for the
murder of Dr. Rulon Allred, leader of a polygamous
group, Church Security moved the Kimballs

temporarily to an apartment in the Hotel Utah. Camilla said, "The apartment is beautiful, but I still feel that I am in prison."

He had assumed he knew what it might be like to be President of the Church, but he had had no idea of the extra stress in living in a fishbowl and in bearing ultimate earthly responsibility for the welfare of three and a third million Church members. The organizational demands on his time were incredible, but he did not want to be isolated from the people. Once when the Twelve reported their visits to distant stakes, Spencer reported, "I spent Saturday and Sunday visiting the sick and the homebound."

On New Year's Day when the family had gathered for dinner, four teenage boys rang the bell at his home, wanting to meet President Kimball. He invited them in and visited, then posed with them for pictures. When he learned they had not eaten, he asked Camilla if she would prepare food for them. A member of his family later commented, "Was all of that really necessary?" He replied, "I belong to all the people, not just to my family."

Long practice of unselfishness made it automatic. Spencer had been given a new sweater that Camilla thought not quite right for him and she thought their son might use it. She said, "Could we give Andy one of your sweaters?" and without hesitation Spencer started to unbutton the sweater he was wearing.

Judge Whitaker, head of the BYU motion picture studio, and a crew spent the morning in Spencer's office shooting some footage. At noon Spencer invited the men to go with him to the Church cafeteria for lunch. As they got in line the hostess saw them and said, "President Kimball, why don't you let me take you and your guests to the dining room and we'll serve you there, rather than have you stand in line." But he said, "No, thank you. We'll wait." Then he turned to the men and asked, "You don't mind, do you?" They did not mind. When they came to the stack of trays, Spencer put napkin and silverware on trays and passed them back to each person in the group before he helped himself.

Traditionally the Church President headed various corporations through which the Church did business. Spencer delegated most of these responsibilities to others so that he could concentrate on other things. He sought to reach out to more of the people, both institutionally and personally. He began announcing new and smaller temples to be built all over the world, first in Sao Paulo, then Tokyo, then dozens more. He held a series of thirty-eight solemn assemblies for instructing Church leaders. He increased area conferences from just one each year to many each year until he had been everywhere in the world where there were concentrations of Saints.

In 1975 Adney Y. Komatsu, the first non-Caucasian General Authority, became an Assistant to the Twelve. In October that year President Kimball activated the First Quorum of the Seventy. Among those called to that quorum were Charles Didier, of Belgium, and George P. Lee, a Navajo, and soon thereafter General Authorities representing half a dozen other nations. Additional important administrative changes followed, including an inactive status for elderly or ill General Authorities and the status of temporary General Authority.

His personal style was warm. Elder Didier moved into a house next door to the Kimballs. The first person to knock on his door was Spencer, bringing a greeting and a cantaloupe.

The neighbor on the other side liked to come out and visit with Spencer whenever Spencer was out in the yard. The neighbor's wife said, "President Kimball deserves a little privacy. You shouldn't impose on him to have to visit with you all the time." So he stopped going out. After about ten days Spencer appeared at the door with a plate of cookies. "I'm here to apologize," he said. "What for?" "I don't know.

It is to make up for whatever I did that made you mad at me. You used to come out to visit me, but now you seem to be avoiding me."

Once he was resting on the back seat of the car while being driven by a member of the Church security staff. Suddenly he sat bolt upright, took off his glasses, and looked intently at the driver. "Is this your first family?" he asked. "No," the driver answered, puzzled, "I was married before, many years ago." Spencer lay down again, then sat up and asked, "How is your son?" The driver had only daughters by his second marriage, as Spencer knew, and he replied, "I don't know. I have not been allowed to see him since he was just a baby." Spencer said, "You have good things to look forward to," and lay down. The driver wondered why the President had been looking through his personnel file. When he asked his supervisor about it later he learned that the President had not seen his file. "Then how did he know about my family situation?" "He's the prophet." About a week later the driver heard a knock at his door and a young man of about twenty asked his name and then said, "I am your son." The son had found his way back. When the driver excitedly reported the event to President Kimball, Spencer said, "You have still more good things to look forward to."

His leadership style was simple, unassuming. When the missionary committee, having before it the application of one of his grandsons, asked,

"President Kimball, have you any suggestions where he should be sent?" he answered, "Yes, wherever the Lord wants him to serve." Later, when signing the letter of call, President Kimball added a postscript, "I'm proud of you. Grandpa."

Early one morning Marvin J. Ashton's telephone rang. "Marvin?" "Yes, President Kimball?" "Could I come up and see you?" "President Kimball, if you want to see me, I will be right down." "Would you do that?" When Elder Ashton got to his office Spencer handed him a letter and asked, "How would you answer this?" He made some suggestions. "Thank you. I agree," said Spencer.

Elaine Cannon, president of the Young Women, stood waiting for an elevator in the Church office building one morning. As the elevator arrived, two security men appeared suddenly and in an official way held the door open. Unaccustomed to such treatment, she turned and saw Spencer and Arthur Haycock coming. She stepped back out of the way and let them on the elevator. After Spencer got on the elevator and turned around, he saw her standing there waiting for the next elevator. "Good morning, Elaine," he said. "Good morning, President Kimball." "Aren't you going to get on?" "Well, I didn't think I was supposed to under the circumstances." "Aren't you going up?" "Yes." "How do you intend to get there? If you're going up, you'd better get on."

One of the practices Spencer encouraged in his sermons was the keeping of personal journals and the writing of family history. He saw that as part of the religious obligation to do genealogical research and strengthen family ties. For most of his life he had been a regular journal keeper, with a whole shelf of black looseleaf binders in which he kept his typewritten entries, often illustrated with photographs or pictures cut out of magazines. His published biography, *Spencer W. Kimball,* relied heavily on those extensive journals for information. People learned from that source that he was a real person, not some perfect person completely unlike them.

In the winter of 1976 President Kimball arrived in Samoa for the first of nine area conferences in the Pacific. He and Camilla both fell suddenly ill, with high fever and nausea, later diagnosed as viral pneumonia. Though miserable, they did not consider turning back. As they arrived in New Zealand by plane his fever broke and Spencer managed a television interview and a luncheon with the prime minister. Then right after the two important events his fever returned and Spencer went back to bed.

For the Saturday evening cultural program, Spencer asked President N. Eldon Tanner to represent him because of his illness. During the evening he woke

with a start, his fever broken again. He asked Dr.
Nelson, who sat by him, "What time was the program
to begin?" "At seven o'clock, President Kimball."
"What time is it now?" "Almost seven." "Tell Sister
Kimball we're going!" As they drove into the stadium,
just after the opening prayer, the crowd erupted in a
deafening shout. The young man who had just offered
the opening prayer had pleaded, "We three
thousand New Zealand youth have gathered here to
sing and dance for thy prophet. Wilt thou heal him
and deliver him here!"

Later in the year, after an area conference in
Denmark, the President and several Apostles went to
visit the chapel where the famous Thorvaldsen statues
of Christ and his Apostles stand. Though the chapel
was closed for renovation, the custodian was kind
enough to show them around. President Kimball
testified to the custodian that the men who stood
before him were living Apostles. He said, "The keys of
priesthood authority which Peter held, I hold today."
The custodian wept, "Today I have been in the
presence of servants of God."

A famous Protestant minister related to his radio
audience an encounter with Spencer. He had been
struggling with a personal problem for weeks when he
came to Salt Lake City to speak and was invited to
meet the First Presidency. After getting an impression
of the men he met, he asked, "President Kimball,

would you bless me?" "You mean you want me to give you a blessing such as I give our people?" "Yes." So the First Presidency laid hands on his head and gave him a blessing, that the Lord would be near and guide him. His emotions touched, he had a wondrous feeling and said, "Sir, He is here. I feel His presence." Then as he walked outside into the crisp morning and looked up at the mountains he suddenly felt his burden lift and realized the solution to his difficulty.

As the Church grew in numbers and influence it also became exposed to criticism. Its opposition to the proposed "Equal Rights Amendment" to the United States Constitution drew heavy fire. In a 1976 statement the First Presidency expressed its view that even though women deserved better treatment in employment and other ways, the ERA was not the best way to deal with the problem. Spencer was glad for opportunities to demonstrate his regard for women by participating in the dedication of the Relief Society Monument to Women in Nauvoo and by convening the first general women's meeting in the Church, sent by closed circuit communication to fourteen hundred locations.

His concern was not just for public show. Right after Spencer had called James E. Faust to fill a vacancy in the Quorum of the Twelve, Elder Faust went to conduct a committee meeting with some other General Authorities. In a few minutes his secretary interrupted the meeting with a call from Spencer, who asked, "Have you called your Ruth?" "No, President. I had this meeting and haven't had time." "I think you'd better call your wife."

As the sweep of his responsibilities widened it became harder for the aging president to reach out to individuals, however much he tried. Sometimes the crush of affectionate members alarmed those concerned for his safety. The first of eight area conferences in 1977 in Latin America brought twenty-five thousand Saints together in Mexico City from as far as fifteen hundred miles away. He described his vision for the Lamanites, that they would flourish and take an important place in their communities. At the conclusion of the conference the congregation burst into spontaneous singing and waved white handkerchiefs. There was no way he could greet such a crowd. But between conference meetings in La Paz, Bolivia, at 12,500-foot altitude where visitors gasped for breath, Spencer said to General Authorities with him, "I think the people want to be closer. Can't we do something like shaking hands with them after the conference?" The others said, "That's too much, President. We don't think you should do that." But he urged, "These people came long distances to meet us. I don't see how we can disappoint them." He asked the four of them how they would vote and got four no's. He thanked them for their advice. Then as he concluded his remarks at the end of the conference he said to the two thousand people in attendance, "If those of you who would like to do so would line up in an orderly fashion after the meeting, we would like to shake your hands before we leave." After the prayer people poured out of the congregation. For perhaps two hours the Brethren stood and greeted the people, every child and adult who wished it.

The growing diversity in the Church was illustrated by the fact that in Bogota an Indian district president from Ecuador, in sandals and white linen trousers and with braided hair hanging down his back, offered one of the prayers. It seemed fitting that Spencer spoke on the Savior's disapproval of class distinctions.

The heads of five countries received him on this one trip, giving him a chance to explain what the Church stands for, particularly in terms of honesty, industry, commitment to family, and loyalty to country. Though he understood their importance, tasks of this sort always distressed him because of the political landmines scattered about. His secretary said, "He would do anything for the Kingdom, even this." It was a long way from Thatcher, Arizona.

On a visit to Canada Spencer had a red-coated Mountie as a security escort, who described their encounter: "We are taught in the Mounties to respect a privacy zone of four to five feet while escorting a VIP. Dignitaries . . . expect respect and distance. But when I walked beside President Kimball I was overwhelmed with his humility. As we walked down the stairs he put his arm through mine, breaking right through the privacy zone. He patted me on the hand like a father would his son. I almost blubbered right out loud while escorting him."

On an airplane a clean-cut young man asked, "Are you President Kimball?" and Spencer engaged him in conversation for a half hour, twice leaning over to kiss him on the cheek. The boy dabbed at tears in his eyes. The conversation ended when the plane arrived in Salt Lake City. In the airport someone who had observed the incident said to the boy, "You must be LDS, to have spent so much time with the prophet." "No, I'm not," he replied. "I've studied about the Church and had seen pictures of President Kimball, so I recognized him when I saw him." "What did you talk about?" "He asked me to be baptized." "Are you going to do it?" "It is hard to refuse when a prophet asks you to be baptized."

I n August Spencer went to Europe to set apart a new temple presidency in Switzerland and to visit the Minister of Religion in Poland. While he waited a few days for his appointment in Poland, Spencer asked that meetings be arranged in the Italian missions. The time was not fully scheduled and he asked Arthur

Haycock, his secretary, why. Arthur explained that they were just trying to save his strength. Spencer responded, "I know you're trying to save me, but I don't want to be saved, I want to be exalted!" Arthur arranged extra meetings.

David Kennedy had worked for a long time to obtain legal recognition of the Church by the Communist government in Poland and finally obtained it. Legal status did not mean missionaries could go to Poland, but it did mean that meetings could be held for the few members there, and it meant freer communication. When Spencer and his party arrived in Poland the Communist Minister of Religion received them respectfully, even refraining from smoking or drinking in their presence.

The minister arranged a day of seeing places of historic interest for them, and late in the evening, after a private choral concert in the cathedral, he took them to the adjoining private residence of the Catholic Archbishop of Warsaw. Camilla first thought it was just one more building to look at, and when she saw the long flight of stairs she asked if she could just sit down to wait for the others and save her arthritic knees. Suddenly four priests appeared with a chair. They were going to carry her upstairs in it. Embarrassed, she rushed up the stairs, aching knees and all. She was doubly embarrassed to find that the archbishop had a table of refreshments waiting for them.

The next morning early the small group gathered in a downtown park under an overcast sky for a dedicatory prayer before they left Poland. Then, as Spencer concluded his prayer, the sun came out.

Back in Salt Lake City that fall, during a meeting Spencer suddenly had great difficulty in breathing and was rushed to the hospital. Dr. Nelson, who had performed his heart surgery, came to Spencer's room and found him appearing deathly ill. At his request, Dr. Nelson gave him a blessing, in which he felt inspired to promise speedy recovery even before the doctors could diagnose the condition, so that Spencer could return to his work without missing any significant appointment. The next day the diagnostic tests were inconclusive and Spencer felt much better. He left the hospital that evening and next day flew to Canada to help install a new temple presidency, having missed no significant appointment.

Another time Dr. Nelson received a call to see Spencer, because he was feeling sick. Though the doctor could find no physical explanation, Spencer was clearly ill. On inquiring whether anything upsetting had happened during the day, he learned that two young LDS missionaries in Texas had been murdered by a lunatic. It became apparent that

Spencer's concern for the families of those missionaries had made him physically ill.

In the spring of 1978 Camilla sensed that something was weighing heavily on Spencer's mind, but she did not know what it was and knew his feelings about confidentiality too well to ask. She thought perhaps it was a serious problem with one of the General Authorities, but she could only wonder. On June 8, the telephone rang as Camilla worked tending flowers in the garden. Her daughter, Olive Beth, asked excitedly, "Have you heard the news?" "What news?" "About the revelation. It is on the radio and television that Dad has received a revelation that all worthy men can receive the priesthood!" After delight at the news, her next thought was, "Will the Church accept it?

Will people fall away?" She went into her bedroom to weep and pray in thanks and relief. She now understood that Spencer must have been worried about whether the revelation would cause dissension in the Church, as Wilford Woodruff's 1890 manifesto had done. But their worry was unnecessary.

The electrifying news that worthy Church members of all races could receive the full blessings of priesthood and temple caused nearly universal rejoicing in the Church, both for the extension of blessings and because it demonstrated the basic principle of continuing revelation. The General Authorities were asked not to elaborate, but to let the announcement of the revelation speak for itself. Nothing so dramatic as this revelation had happened in the Church in generations.

Within a few days Joseph Freeman, Jr., received the Melchizedek Priesthood and could go with his wife and two sons to be sealed as a family in the temple. In August, Marcus Martins, the first black missionary called after the revelation, began serving in his home country of Brazil, and his father soon began service in a stake presidency.

With his deep concern about people, President Kimball felt humbly grateful to have been God's instrument to open these doors. But after the burst of great excitement, he turned back to the business of building the Kingdom little by little.

In the summer of 1979 Spencer had a frightening dizzy spell that the doctor diagnosed as a tiny stroke. When Spencer complained, "I have no balance," Dr. Nelson reassured him, "That will pass." Spencer responded, wryly, "What won't?" A second such incident got him thinking about dying. "We have our bags packed," he explained. "We're ready to go." His eyesight faded, too, so that in the Toronto area conference for the first time he turned his talk over to Arthur Haycock to read.

He needed help in walking. It appeared that he was sliding rapidly downwards. When he went to BYU to speak to twenty thousand students, he had to ask BYU president Dallin Oaks to finish reading his talk. But his sense of humor had not left him; at a lunch BYU provided for the Kimball family, Spencer expressed thanks for "the delightful repast. We're so glad to be able to eat with our family without having to provide the food."

The next day his weakness became so pronounced that he was hospitalized for tests. His condition was diagnosed as a subdural hematoma (blood and fluid inside the skull, pressing on the brain), requiring emergency surgery. Providentially his anticoagulant medicine had been stopped in preparation for a scheduled eye operation, so that the brain operation could proceed without fear of uncontrolled bleeding. Dr. Sorensen drilled a burr hole the size of a pencil through the skull two inches above his right ear, and the fluid, under great pressure, spurted out about two feet.

The doctor predicted that perhaps President Kimball would be able to attend October conference, but felt sure he would not be able to participate. In fact, however, Spencer spoke five times. He had once said to his doctor, who urged him to slow down, "My dear doctor, if you knew what I know about the timetable of the Lord, if you knew the commitments that I have been required to make in the sacred office that I hold, you would find that there is no alternative."

Shortly after conference, despite his frailty, he travelled to Jerusalem. Members of the Church had raised a million dollars by private subscription to establish a garden for the city of Jerusalem on the Mount of Olives in commemoration of the dedicatory prayer of Orson Hyde. On his way to Israel, Spencer went to Arab Egypt, where government officials greeted him, and in his remarks and dedicatory prayer at the Orson Hyde Garden he specified his concern for all the children of Abraham, Arab and Jew alike.

About Thanksgiving time pressure built up again inside his skull, requiring a second operation similar to the first. This time the operation required his missing area conferences in New Zealand and Australia. As he was recovering from the anesthetic he showed his great need for affection. He fancied that he had attended a dinner for a thousand people and, to his distress, no one had set a place for him. No one said even, "We're glad to have you here, President." For one who loved people so much, nothing could be more saddening than to be excluded by them.

In reality, people loved and honored him. Arthur Haycock said, as Spencer's eighty-fifth birthday approached and Spencer objected to the plans that had been made, "President, they're going to have the birthday party whether you're there or not, so I think it might be a nice thing if you'd come and enjoy it, too." "Maybe we'd better," Spencer smiled. One night the Tabernacle was crowded for a program and the next night a banquet for two thousand people in the Hotel Utah honored him. Among other gifts, he received portraits of his father and mother. Sometimes, as he grew old, he thought about the joy of being reunited with his parents.

Area conferences resumed and he participated again. Because his eyes were bad, he had his talks typed in capital letters four times normal size so that he could read them. In April Conference 1981 President Kimball reported that since October he had travelled fifty thousand miles, holding area conferences in the Orient and in the Pacific islands and flying to South America and Puerto Rico and the Dominican Republic.

But numbers could never tell the whole story. For example, after a meeting in Santo Domingo, he had gone to bed when a hundred members, packed in an overloaded bus, arrived terribly late, many in tears, because their bus had broken down. After all their travel they would have to turn right around to return for work the next day, so Arthur Haycock woke Spencer and asked whether he would be willing to send a personal greeting to them. More than that, the President dressed and met with them for an hour, delivering the same message to this group that he had presented in the earlier meeting.

Spencer said to Elder Ashton, "Marvin, I'd like you to take me to visit the Utah State Prison." "President, I don't want you to go to the prison; I am afraid for your safety. There are some men confined there who would like to attract the attention they would get by hurting you." Spencer accepted his advice. But about two months later Elder Ashton decided that a visit to the new prison chapel, then under construction, might allow Spencer to visit the prison but stay outside the dangerous area. In the warden's office Spencer met with two prisoners who had helped with construction of the prison chapel. Elder Ashton turned to Spencer. "Would you like to say a few words to these men?" They looked down, expecting a lecture. When one raised his head Spencer looked into his eyes and said, "Tell me about your mother." Tears came to the man's eyes as he talked about his mother. And Spencer then asked the other man about his father and family.

When the press came in, one of the inmates said, "Mr. Kimball, could I have my picture taken with you?" Spencer responded, "I'd be glad to. Why don't I stand between you two and have our picture taken?" Afterward Spencer thanked them.

With age and illness he clearly slowed down, but he had already set many things in motion that would come to fruition. A new edition of the standard works became available, a project he had encouraged for a number of years. Later the Book of Mormon received a new subtitle: "Another Testament of Jesus Christ." A new Church museum took shape.

In May 1981 the First Presidency issued a statement critical of arms buildup in the world, specifically opposing the basing of MX missiles in the Utah-Nevada desert. And partly in response to this, President Reagan referred the entire proposal back to the military for further study.

Spencer's heartbeat slowed to a dangerous level, and he needed a pacemaker to regularize his heartbeat at sixty-six times per minute, but he postponed it until after he had performed the temple wedding for a granddaughter. Then he went to the hospital for installation.

A reporter once asked him, "Do you ever worry about working too hard, killing yourself?" He replied, "A little, but not very much—not enough to stop."

The University of Utah conferred on both Spencer and Camilla Kimball honorary doctoral degrees in 1981. The citation for him emphasized his role in helping make the Church international and universal, with indirect reference to the revelation on priesthood. Camilla's citation stressed her exemplary life, particularly her promotion of education and of personal growth for women.

In July 1981, with all three members of the First Presidency ailing, President Kimball called Elder Gordon B. Hinckley to be a third counselor. Shortly afterward, Spencer's strength declined sharply. A brain scan showed a third subdural hematoma in the same area as before. This time more than a burr hole was needed; Dr. Sorensen removed a five square inch oval of bone from Spencer's forehead and after removing fluid and scar tissue wired the bone flap back in place.

This time, as often before, Spencer kissed the hands of his doctors as they took care of him. Recovery this time progressed very slowly. Rumors made their appointed rounds—the president had suffered a stroke, he had had two heart attacks, he was totally incapacitated, he lay in a coma. Occasionally the sense of humor that helped him survive so many problems still surfaced. One nurse asked teasingly, "President Kimball, can you tell me when the Second Coming will be?" He said, "Why? Are you ready?"

He was determined to get well. When he suffered a stress ulcer and nearly bled to death, a nurse came in to give an infusion of blood. She tried for a half hour to find a vein that would receive the large needle. She said, placatingly, "I guess you don't want this, do you." He roused enough to say, almost fiercely, "I *do* want it."

Because it was more convenient for his counselors and easier to care for him physically, Spencer and Camilla moved into an apartment near the office until he was able to recover fully.

He did recover enough to carry on some of his responsibilities, but not enough to return to his home to live. He continued in fragile health. He suffered a painful partial collapse of a vertebra, he had an abdominal hernia, he once lapsed into a coma for four hours, his eyesight faded to almost nothing, he had glaucoma, he slept poorly at night and might then fall asleep even in the middle of a meal, fluid retention required a salt-free diet, skin cancers had to be removed, one fall resulted in a cut forehead and a black eye, another fall required seven stitches, he suffered a minor stroke, a toothache required a root canal job, and he suffered periodically from arthritis. There seemed no end of problems, but he bore them patiently. Camilla, too, suffered from ulcers and severe arthritis, and when she broke her hip she had to have it replaced with an artificial joint.

Occasional flashes of wit brightened the atmosphere. His daughter-in-law said, "Last week I was complaining that our zucchini was not doing well, but now the vines are growing fine." Spencer quipped, "You should have complained sooner." And one day as a nurse tried to shave him with an electric shaver, she worked for several minutes, back and forth, around and around, with no results. As he saw her puzzled, Spencer said puckishly, "Perhaps it would work better if you took the cap off."

Despite his problems, it seemed that every time general conference approached he received a new surge of energy and could attend most conference sessions, but he had to rely on others to carry the work forward. He spoke for the last time in public in April conference 1982, but even that brief talk represented a struggle.

His influence continued to be felt, despite his relative inactivity, for the programs he had helped initiate had their own momentum. After the death of N. Eldon Tanner, President Hinckley assumed major responsibility for conducting the affairs of the First Presidency, but he was always careful to acknowledge that he conferred with and acted with the approval of the President. Serious weakness and short-term problems alternated with periods of relative strength for Spencer, but he dressed each day and was usually able to attend the weekly meetings in the temple with his counselors and the Twelve. He had little to say, but he was there, enduring to the end, despite a tired, worn body. He once said, "My life is like my shoes, to be worn out in service."

People sometimes wondered why the Lord would preserve Spencer's life when he could no longer offer active leadership. Perhaps the Lord wanted to offer the Church an example of love, humility, and enduring to the end.

In one of the meetings the Apostles came in turn to offer greeting. Elder Ashton, knowing that the aged prophet had difficulty in seeing, said to him,

"President Kimball, I am Marvin Ashton." Spencer took his hand, paused, and then finally said softly, "Marv Ashton, I love you." That was all.

Elaine Cannon said, "For the first time in my life I think I understand about Christ's love as I watch President Kimball deal with people. One of the nicest things about him is that he isn't even aware how marvelous he is."

Spencer once said, "I still wonder what the Lord was thinking about, making a little country boy like me President of his Church, unless he knew that I didn't have any sense and would just keep on working." No short man ever had a longer stride.